D1002321

earthwise

A GUIDE TO HOPEFUL CREATION CARE

EDITION 3

earthwise

A GUIDE TO HOPEFUL CREATION CARE

Calvin B. DeWitt

FAITH
ALIVE®
Christian Resources

Grand Rapids, Michigan

Cover design: Pete Euwema
Cover art: SuperStock

Earthwise: A Guide to Hopeful Creation Care, © 2011 (Third Edition) by Faith Alive Christian Resources, Grand Rapids, Michigan. (Earlier editions of *Earthwise,* © 1994, 2007 by Faith Alive Christian Resources.) All rights reserved. With the exception of brief excerpts for review purposes, no part of this book may be reproduced in any manner whatsoever without written permission from the publisher. For information or questions about use of copyrighted material please contact Permissions, Faith Alive Christian Resources, 2850 Kalamazoo Ave. SE, Grand Rapids, MI 49560; phone: 1-800-333-8300; fax: 616-726-1164; email: permissions@faithaliveresources.org.

Printed in the United States of America.

We welcome your comments. Call us at 1-800-333-8300 or email us at editors@faithaliveresources.org.

Library of Congress Cataloging-in-Publication Data
DeWitt, Calvin B.
    Earthwise ; a guide to hopeful creation care / by Calvin B. DeWitt. — 3rd ed.
      p. cm.
    Includes bibliographical references.
    ISBN 978-1-59255-672-4
    1. Human ecology—Religious aspects—Christianity. 2. Human ecology—Biblical teaching. I. Title.
    BT695.5.D49 2011
    261.8'8—dc22
           2011006567

5 4 3 2 1

contents

epigraph

The earth was given to man, with this condition, that he should occupy himself in its cultivation. . . . The custody of the garden was given in charge to Adam, to show that we possess the things which God has committed to our hands, on the condition that, being content with the frugal and moderate use of them, we should take care of what shall remain. Let him who possesses a field, so partake of its yearly fruits, that he may not suffer the ground to be injured by his negligence, but let him endeavor to hand it down to posterity as he received it, or even better cultivated. Let him so feed on its fruits, that he neither dissipates it by luxury, nor permits it to be marred or ruined by neglect. Moreover, that this economy, and this diligence, with respect to those good things which God has given us to enjoy, may flourish among us; let everyone regard himself as the steward of God in all things which he possesses. Then he will neither conduct himself dissolutely, nor corrupt by abuse those things which God requires to be preserved.

—John Calvin on Genesis 2:15;
Commentary on Genesis, 1554

foreword

Though he probably has not known this, Calvin DeWitt has been my mentor. I have wanted to make a difference with my life. I have wanted to make a servant's impact for God upon all his creation. And for that I have needed great teachers.

Cal DeWitt has everything to recommend him as a great teacher. He has advanced training in the sciences of which he speaks. He has studied Scripture with his heart and soul as well as his mind. Cal is also respected highly by his peers. He is a cofounder of the leading evangelical network on the environment (Evangelical Environmental Network), and he was the founding director of an institute for environmental studies (Au Sable Institute). Cal is personally intrigued and delighted by God's creation—and has been so from his boyhood. His students revere him not only for his knowledge but also for his integrity. And, besides all that, Cal's work is fun to read.

That's what else I needed: a good textbook. I entered into the advocacy of creation care through the recommendation of other evangelical leaders. I did not know much about the field, but I love to study. I am a pastor, so I was not reading just for me but also for thousands who listen to me. Therefore, I had to be very careful about my reference material. Dr. DeWitt to my rescue! I read *Earthwise* as one of my resource books, and I thought, "How could I have missed this as an important part of following and worshiping God?"

I challenge you to learn from Cal DeWitt (with me), and we will benefit others together. The care of God's creation is not just a way to honor the Creator, although it is that. The care of God's creation is not just a way to love your neighbor (and grandchildren) as you love yourself, although it is that too. The care of God's creation is not just another way to obey God's command to cultivate and keep the earth, though it is also that too. The care of creation is a crucial issue. The way we address it could mean life or death for millions of people around the world. We can help protect those least able to cope with environmental degradation. They are among the "least of these" whom Jesus specifically taught about in Matthew 25.

So this is more than a textbook, and Cal DeWitt is more than a teacher. This is a book of life and a book of love. This is a book that will make your life count more for the benefit of others. This is a book that will help you love the natural world that fascinated you as a child. This is a book that will help you love your neighbor in a practical way.

Read this book and you will be different. So will the world.

—Dr. Joel C. Hunter, Senior Pastor, Northland
Community Church, Orlando, Florida, 2007

Editor's note: This Foreword first appeared in the second edition of *Earthwise*. A member of the United States President's Advisory Council on Faith-Based and Neighborhood Partnerships and of the board of directors of the National Association of Evangelicals, Joel Hunter has helped raise awareness of environmental concerns through his work for the Evangelical Climate Initiative, through preaching and speaking engagements and media interviews, and in his book *A New Kind of Conservative* (Regal Books, 2008).

using this book
Author's Preface to the Third Edition

L iving in harmony with creation and sharing the deep joy of such living is the theme of this book—and this objective is for anyone and everyone, for we are all part of the earth and the environment we live in. In this new edition of *Earthwise* I am writing not only for people of the Christian faith but for all who wish to understand something of the roots of environmental responsibility and care.

As indicated by John Bascom (1879), an early president of the University of Wisconsin, where I teach, "Christianity has expended many hundred years in incorporating into society" many sentiments that are not soon lost, even "if Christianity is rejected." And among those "sentiments" is Christianity's "stewardship tradition," a major gift to the world. I hope that in engaging with this book my readers who are not of the Christian faith will not be offended by the Christian language I use, but instead may recognize an opportunity to discover how the environment can be seen through the eyes of Christian faith. I greatly appreciate their tolerance, if not appreciation, of a perspective that may differ from that of their own background or tradition.

In the first two editions of this book, I wrote to try to inspire discussion groups in Christian churches, household gatherings, and classes in schools and colleges, urging people to action. Much has happened in the nearly twenty years since publication of the first edition, not only in our understanding of the way the world works and of our human impact on the environment, but also in Christianity as it increasingly rediscovers itself as "a religion and philosophy of creation" (Clarence J. Glacken, 1967). Beyond this rediscovery is a growing appreciation of the influence of Christianity in producing leading "environmentalists" such as George Perkins Marsh, John Muir, Teddy Roosevelt, and Rachel Carson, two of whom memorized the New Testament before they were teenagers. Not too surprisingly, we also have found that ecology—the study of organisms in relationship with their environment—has deep Christian roots.

HOW MIGHT YOU BENEFIT?

In all three editions of this book, I have written not only from my grounding in the natural sciences that came largely from the education and training I received as a scientist, but also from the heritage of my childhood and youth. I know that my heritage is responsible for my becoming a scientist and, more, for becoming a person who continually seeks to develop and sustain a holistic and integrative worldview—a worldview that accords with the way the world works. In this, I embrace not only the pursuit of scientific understanding but also questions regarding "what ought to be" in human life and action and "what we then ought to do" in our life and work. My deepest interest is to achieve as comprehensive and coherent an understanding of how the world works as possible, and in this context to live in harmony with creation and to share the inspiring joy of such living. In pursuing this interest, I am impatient with unscientific methods and speculations, and I continue to work at being fully grounded in what I learn, know, and believe from scholarly colleagues past and present in science and theology, in order to work from the best possible base of knowledge and understanding, within my gifts and capacities, to know who I am and to learn my role in society and creation.

In my journey into science, accompanied and nurtured by my heritage, I am indebted to the upholding Christian community in which I was raised. I know that people have questioned heritages such as mine, that others have abandoned them, and that even more hold wholly different beliefs or nonbeliefs. But all of us know and appreciate that each of us was born and raised at a place and time over which we had no control. None of us is responsible (or can take credit) for his or her own particular heritage.

So I find myself asking, "How might you, with your particular heritage, benefit from reading *Earthwise*, stemming as it does from my particular heritage?"

First, if you share the same or a similar heritage, I expect that you might be inspired to be a faithful steward of creation. Or if your heritage is different from mine, you may find *Earthwise* helpful in understanding the contributions that biblical and theological study bring to environmentalism and ecology, and you may find that exercise helpful in your conversations with people of Christian faith. In addition, if your heritage is Christian and yet has had little to say about God's creation or care for it, I hope you will be uplifted to find that together in *Earthwise* we (re)discover many of the biblical teachings that make up Christianity's "stewardship tradition."

I also realize that you might be reading *Earthwise* as an individual, a member of a study group, or as a member of a college or university class. In that regard I hope that in this book you will find helpful the ideas and suggestions that come from my experience in teaching and learning.

REFLECTIVE JOURNAL

As you engage with *Earthwise* and use it as a primer for thinking and action, I strongly suggest that you obtain a bound journal with blank pages into which you can enter your thoughts, observations, and reflective thinking. Then you can write, in your own style, a collection of "letters to yourself" reflecting on experiences, observations, and ideas that come to mind from reading and reflecting on *Earthwise* and from related matters in your daily life. This might include reflections you have gathered from radio, television, lectures, or sermons; or from a walk or hike, during your travel through town or across the landscape; or from observing or working in a garden; or through discussion or debate with a friend or antagonist. You can keep your reflections to yourself, of course, but you might also enjoy sharing some of your thoughts with others, particularly when they might have something to share with you from their own reflective journals.

INTEGRATIVE NOTEBOOK

Earthwise is a primer, not a "last word," so you might like to do as thousands of my students have done: prepare your own loose-leaf book that helps you build on what you read and study here—and then continue, through the months and years ahead, to assemble and organize materials into an integrated whole. I suggest obtaining a three-ring binder in which you can gather and organize materials on environmental understanding, environmental practice, and creation care. Aim for a careful and meaningful integration of things that inform and inspire you, things you have done,

13

and things you hope to do. Your materials could include brochures, articles, sketches, photos, diagrams, and more.

As you begin, simply insert materials in any order that seems best to you. Then later you may want to reorganize the contents along lines that begin to shape an integrative framework. As the weeks pass, you could consider ways in which reorganization could continue to achieve an ever better integration of readings, thoughts, experiences, and personal practices.

I also suggest that, in time, you open your notebook to others to allow them to make comments and suggestions, and to inspire them to evaluate how you are doing. You can leave your notebook "lying around" on a coffee table or countertop so that friends and guests feel free to open it. It might contain a log of activities, sheets on animals and plants observed, reprints and pages from magazines and newspapers, records of plantings in your garden and of trees and shrubs in your yard, photocopies, and computer printouts. And of course you can organize your notebook again and again. You can use dividers with index tabs and removable labels to help you organize information. At some point you might also want to fit the volume with an attractive cover and a title page that includes your name. A table of contents and a preface describing its origin and purpose can also be helpful. Be as creative as you wish!

TEACHING AND LEARNING CLUB

You might also like to link with four or five other people to study *Earthwise*—and perhaps to share readings from your reflective journals, or to exchange ideas and materials for your three-ring notebooks. See also "A Short Course in Environmental Science" in the Appendix of this book.

When I'm part of a teaching and learning club, I like to find a convenient, friendly corner in a coffee shop to get together regularly. This can be tremendous fun; give it a try! And when you get to the mini-workshop in chapter 5 of this book, your teaching and learning club might just want to become the group that works to implement the results of the workshop in your community, neighborhood, congregation, school, or other group.

SHARING THE JOY OF HARMONIOUS LIVING

When you reach a point in your study of *Earthwise* at which you ask, "What can I do? What must I do?"—then you no doubt will also take action to live in harmony with creation. Beyond "doing something" personally, there is also the invigorating work of sharing with others the joy of such living. After all, caring for creation and enjoying life lived in harmony with the way the world works should not be kept to ourselves!

So you will want to ask, "Where are the opportunities? Where are the openings? What are the possibilities?" What might you do, how might you participate, in bringing good news and good practice to every creature? You will not only want to discover or refresh your passion for creation care; you will also want to "put wheels under" that passion!

As you do, may you also grow in realizing the joyful results of praying, "Your kingdom come, your will be done, on earth . . ." (Matt. 6:10)!

introduction

I have been in love with the Creator since my childhood and have been inspired and awed by God's creation for well over half a century. I gained an early appreciation for God's creatures from caring for and keeping animals in the backyard zoo of my childhood and youth.

I am a teacher, and I love to teach about the wonders of the beautiful life that envelops the earth. From my first teaching assignment at age 16—a course in herpetology for young people at the Grand Rapids (Mich.) Public Museum—I went on to teach thousands of college and university students (and nearly every other person I've ever met), helping them to develop a sense of awe and wonder for God's world. Like the great Teacher—my model—I too like to teach on field trips! And I am a continuous student, learning from the "university of creation" and from God's holy Word.

One Sunday evening when I was in my teens, I overheard my uncle ask my dad a question about me: "Shouldn't you help Cal do something more important than this—something that will help him get a job?" My dad was guiding him down the basement stairs to see my birds and fish while my mom and aunt prepared after-church coffee and goodies in the kitchen above. As they approached the door to my aviary and aquaria, I heard my dad softly reply that he thought I was doing just fine. You see, my dad had told me earlier to keep doing what I loved to do; that would mean I would do it very well—and that meant eventually someone would even pay me for it. In this—his rendition of Matthew 6:33—he proved to be ever so right! I now get paid for what I love to do. My profession is caring for God's creation and helping others to do so.

From the subtitle, *A Guide to Hopeful Creation Care,* it would seem reasonable to conclude that this book is rooted in care for the natural environment and ecology. But my own vocation—and "where I'm coming from"—stems from a time long before anyone heard or taught much about "the environment" or "environmental-ism." So while this book is a response to environmental issues of today, its *root*—and the *root* of my vocation—is in my delight in God's creation. My motivation is summed up pretty well by Psalm 111:2: "Great are the works of the LORD; they are pondered by all who delight in them." What a wonderful world God has given us! It's a world so convicting of God's divinity and everlasting power that everyone is without an excuse for not knowing something about God from his delightful creation (Rom. 1:20). Our delight calls for our study, our seeking out, and our full investigation of this marvelous creation!

This book aims both to lighten the load we carry and to urge us to joyful, redeeming action in and with God's amazing world. It will not pile on guilt. God knows that we, along with the rest of humanity, are guilty, "for all have sinned and fall short of the glory of God" (Rom. 3:23). But ours is not to grovel in polluted gutters or to wring our hands over our sins. Instead, we are called to go about reclaiming creation for our Lord, knowing that "the earth is the LORD's, and everything in it" (Ps. 24:1) and that we may eagerly do so out of joyful gratitude for God's great gift of salvation.

Even as we begin, we are uplifted by the knowledge of God's rule, of God's loving gift of Jesus—through whom the world was made and in whom "all things hold together" (Col. 1:17). Jesus Christ is the one given by God to reconcile all things to himself (Col. 1:20). We know he is the one we must follow. Jesus is our best example of practicing dominion and stewardship.

So let's join together not only to explore the dark recesses of creation's degradations but also to resurface into the Bible's teach-ings on creation's care and keeping—and then to ascend into the joyful stewardship of the faithful children of God!

—Calvin B. ("Cal") DeWitt

01

Seven Provisions for Creation[1]

I was born and raised in the city of Grand Rapids, Michigan, and for nearly forty years now I have inhabited the great Waubesa Marsh in Wisconsin.

In many ways it is easier to learn of the workings of God's creation in this wetland ecosystem, but the city of my youth also provided a wonderful place to learn creation's lessons. With my brother and sister I felt the drifting wetness of torrential rains and gentle drizzles as we swung on a suspended canvas swing in the shelter of our front porch. One day a tornado's immense funnel cloud roared menacingly over the roof of the nearby Baxter Laundry. On summer evenings we heard the noisy "zzbbrrraaaaaaaaaaannnggggg!" of nighthawks breaking the silence of the night sky as they pulled out of their dramatic plunging dives. We also watched bats zig-zagging in flight around our corner streetlight, keeping insects in check. And then there was Mrs. Lockhart's Dutchman's pipe—a climbing vine with heart-shaped leaves—on which pipevine swallowtail caterpillars ate away with her reluctant approval. These caterpillars eventually

[1] A full treatment of the provisions of the biosphere, in addition to a description of environmental abuses and needed response, can be found in Richard T. Wright and Bernard J. Nebel, *Environmental Science: Toward a Sustainable Future*, 10th edition (Englewood Cliffs, N.J.: Prentice-Hall, 2007).

transformed into magnificent butterflies that fluttered around the neighborhood or flopped around as they emerged as captives in my mother's canning jars. Better still were my bike rides to the dump at the edge of town and into the countryside, where I could find frogs, salamanders, snakes, and turtles. I brought home many of these treasures to my backyard zoo where I could study them for hours and days on end.

There was no question in my mind about the reason for all this wonderful life. What I was learning from these beautiful creatures was fully consistent with what I was hearing from sermons in church and from lessons at Baldwin Christian School. All these were God's creatures, works of the Master, the Creator in whom all creatures great and small—his Master-pieces—lived and moved and had their being. They were among the ones we sang about each Sunday: "Praise God . . . all creatures here below"!

Day after day this world opened new lessons about God's creatures and presented new things for which to give God praise. The psalms I sang in church beautifully complemented what I was learning in creation. Remember how Psalm 148 goes, for example? This is the way we sang it:

> Hallelujah, praise Jehovah,
> From the heavens praise His Name;
> Praise Jehovah in the highest,
> All His angels, praise proclaim.
> All His hosts, together praise Him,
> Sun and moon and stars on high;
> Praise Him, O ye heavens of heavens,
> And ye floods above the sky.

And then, in the next stanza:

> Let them praises give Jehovah,
> They were made at His command;
> Them forever He established,
> His decree shall ever stand.
> From the earth, O praise Jehovah,
> All ye seas, ye monsters all,
> Fire and hail and snow and vapors,
> Stormy winds that hear His call.

Then we burst forth with everything we had as we sang of trees, frogs, turtles, elephants, Holsteins, Jerseys, birds, kings, and relatives and neighbors:

> All ye fruitful trees and cedars,
> All ye hills and mountains high,
> Creeping things and beasts and cattle,
> Birds that in the heavens fly,
> Kings of earth, and all ye people,
> Princes great, earth's judges all;
> Praise His Name, young men and maidens,
> Aged men and children small.
>
> Let them praises give Jehovah
> For His Name alone is high,
> And His glory is exalted,
> And His glory is exalted,
> And His glory is exalted,
> Far above the earth and sky.

—Psalter Hymnal, 1959, 1976; 304

Years later on Sunday evenings when friends and neighbors from around our marsh and the nearby city of Madison came together, we often sang that very song. And when we followed our singing with a walk through this wetland, a neighbor shouted, "Birds that in the heavens fly!"

All creation praises God. Of this I am fully convinced. But beyond that, all creation breaks forth with a marvelous testimony—one so powerful that it leaves everyone without excuse for knowing something of God's everlasting power and lordship over all things. I remember in my youth savoring Article 2 of the Belgic Confession because it affirmed, in a deep theological way, the worth of my continuous observation and study of animals and plants in the city, the dump, and the outlying countryside:

Article 2: The Means by Which We Know God

We know him by two means:

First, by the creation, preservation, and government of the universe,

21

since that universe is before our eyes
like a beautiful book
   in which all creatures,
   great and small,
   are as letters
   to make us ponder
   the invisible things of God:
      his eternal power
      and his divinity,
      as the apostle Paul says in Romans 1:20.

All these things are enough to convict men
and to leave them without excuse.

Second, he makes himself known to us more
openly
by his holy and divine Word,
as much as we need in this life,
   for his glory
   and for the salvation of his own.

I knew from this marvelous confession that reading and study of the Bible in my home, school, and church was very important. And—wonderfully!—this confession also affirmed the importance of reading and studying the "beautiful book" of God's creation.

Today the heavens continue to tell the glory of God, and earth's creatures continue to pour forth their testimony to God's eternal power and divine majesty (Ps. 19:1-4).

In early spring Waubesa Marsh bursts forth with extravagant abundance of life. Geese arrive, and soon afterward sandhill cranes wing down, announcing with their clangoring calls the arrival and revival of life on the great marsh.

Why such praise? Why such splendor and rebirth in spring-time? A joyful reading of Psalm 104 helps provide the answer. This psalm celebrates God as the great Provider and masterful Creator. God's provisions for life and breath are everywhere evident. God's provisions are so numerous and interwoven with each other that we cannot begin to give them their proper due.

Yet it is vitally important for us to put these provisions of our Creator into perspective. Bringing all this in through our senses and incorporating it into our mind's eye helps us see more clearly God's "eternal power and divine nature" (Rom. 1:20). And through our study we grow to pour more meaning into our singing of doxologies, as in "Praise God . . . all creatures here below" and "Gloria in excelsis Deo."

Many of us have had awesome experiences in God's creation. Perhaps we have stood at the edge of a great canyon, or at the feet of giant trees in an ancient forest, or in the eye of a great storm. Perhaps we've enjoyed a flowering meadow as the morning mists lifted quietly, and we found ourselves humming "How Great Thou Art." How I wish we could walk together now to a place that would bring forth that song; it would put us into the right frame of mind for understanding God's provisions for creation. Let's open our minds now to the awesome wonder of our Lord's creation!

If at this moment you can put yourself in an environment that calls forth praise to God—do so! Maybe you have a creation-celebrating psalm or recording at your fingertips, or an inspiring view outside your window or in the yard, some flowers on a windowsill, or an open window to let in fresh air. At the very least, shift your position and put your mind in a mood for bringing God praise.

SEVEN PROVISIONS OF THE CREATOR

Let's reflect on seven of God's magnificent provisions for creation. These provisions—many of which are celebrated in Psalm 104—tell something of the remarkable integrity and beauty that have engendered awe, wonder, and respect for the Creator and creation through the ages.

1. Earth's Energy Exchange with the Sun and Space

Our star, the sun, radiates immense energy in all directions, heating whatever is in the path of its rays. This great thermonuclear energy source—the star that brightens earthly life—is a great empowering provision of God's love. It energizes nearly everything we know on earth: green plants and all creatures that eat them, great flows of water and air across the globe, movement of automobiles and aircraft, heating for homes and factories.

Our earth also radiates energy, emitting not visible light but invisible infrared "light"—radiation below the red end of the spectrum. If the energy earth takes in from the sun is greater than energy radiated out by earth into space, the earth's temperature rises. If our earth loses more energy than it gains, it cools. Earth's energy balance—its temperature—needs to be relatively constant for the planet to remain habitable.

Enveloping the earth is its atmosphere. The atmosphere is a protective layer of air situated between us and the sun, and between us and outer space. Among its many functions—like providing the air we breathe—the atmosphere controls energy exchange between the earth and sun and between the earth and outer space. It does this by means of "doorkeeper" gases. Doorkeeper gases—such as carbon dioxide and water vapor—let most of the sun's energy move through the atmosphere to the earth. But these very same gases restrict and delay the flow of energy that the earth radiates into outer space. They do this because they are more transparent to visible light than to infrared radiation. The result is that the earth keeps warm—but not too warm—so that life flourishes. The doorkeeper gases help make a habitable earth.

Window glass in our cars, homes, and greenhouses works similarly. Such glass lets visible light through to the interior but does not let much infrared radiation out. So the inside of our cars, homes, and greenhouses warms up when the sun shines. Because doorkeeper gases act in a way similar to window glass, they also are called "greenhouse gases." In addition, the effect of greenhouse gases being largely transparent to visible light but not to infrared radiation is called "the greenhouse effect." For our earth, this greenhouse effect results in just the right amount of energy leaving the earth to balance the earth's energy gain from the sun. This great provision of God for making the earth habitable for living creatures—including us!—brings joy to our hearts and praise to earth's Maker.

If David or another biblical psalmist had known of this provision, we might have a psalm in our Bible that praises God like this:

> You energize the earth with an outpouring of light;
>> you bathe it with empowering rays.
> You keep the earth warm as with a blanket;
>> you keep its heat near your creatures' hearts.
> Your biosphere flourishes;
>> the earth is upheld by sustaining love.

Not all of the sun's energy supports life, however. It also includes harmful, dangerous, and even deadly radiation—powerful invisible rays above the blue and violet end of the spectrum. Maybe you've seen "black lights" that we can install in electrical light fixtures. They give off no visible light, but they make light-colored clothing and various minerals appear to "glow in the dark." Such "near ultraviolet" light produces radiation immediately above the visible end of the spectrum and is not very dangerous. The next higher level of radiation, however—"far ultraviolet"—is dangerous. When far ultraviolet radiation is absorbed by living and non-living things, not only does it make them warm up, but it transfers such high levels of energy that it ruptures chemical bonds, breaks molecules apart, and disrupts and destroys living tissues. Of particular concern is the breaking of DNA—the genetic blueprint chemical of living things. Damage and breakup of DNA can result in death to cells and microscopic creatures and can affect the instructions given by DNA in ways that produce skin cancer.

But very little ultraviolet radiation ever reaches the earth—and almost no far ultraviolet! It is intercepted in the atmosphere by a "guardian gas" called *ozone*. Sometimes we experience the sharp smell of ozone produced by arcing electric motors or after lightning strikes. This gas can be dangerous for people and other creatures when it occurs in significant quantities near the surface of the earth, and this situation can prompt "ozone alerts" in some large metropolitan areas. In the upper atmosphere, however, ozone is vitally important; the protective "ozone shield" is another of God's remarkable provisions for a habitable earth. If we could collect all the ozone from the upper atmosphere and place it at sea-level atmospheric pressure and at 32 degrees Fahrenheit (0 degrees Celsius), it would be only about one-eighth of an inch (3 mm) thick! And yet that amount of ozone is enough to prevent most of the sun's ultraviolet radiation from penetrating our atmosphere and entering the household of life. That's another reason why God's creatures are able to live on the earth.

If the biblical psalmist had known of this provision by the Creator, we might have a stanza like this in one of the psalms:

The creatures that dwell in the shelter of God's
    providence
  rest in the shadow of the Almighty.
God covers his earth with a protective shield;
  God guards the life he has made to inhabit
    the earth.
How great are your provisions, O Lord!
  You so love your world that you protect its life!

2. Soil Building

Soils build and develop. We learn something of this from gardening as we spade plants back into the soil and add compost to make it richer. This process of soil building also takes place naturally in fields, forests, and wetlands as organic plant and animal matter partially decomposes and accumulates. In addition, soil is produced and enriched by the weathering of rocks and grains of sand.

Soil gets richer and more supportive of life as it interacts with climate, rainfall, and the myriad organisms that live in it. Topsoil builds up, becoming richer in nutrients and more supportive of plant life. Remarkable cycles are involved in this development of soil: the carbon cycle, the water cycle, the nitrogen cycle—to name just a few. These cycles contribute to a veritable symphony of processes that bring bare landscapes—even bare rock—eventually to support a rich and diverse fabric of living things.

Soil building teaches patience. It can take a hundred years to form an inch (2.54 cm) of topsoil—and yet more often only an eighth-inch (3 mm) of soil is produced in that amount of time! The dynamic fabric of roots, soil organisms, and soils that bind together the surface of the biosphere makes one stand in awe of God's patience as Provider. For "with the Lord a day is like a thousand years, and a thousand years are like a day" (2 Pet. 3:8).

Where does this soil building happen? Everywhere! In the cool of temperate zones this soil building produces our prairie and woodland soils. Farther toward the north pole it produces soils in boreal forests. And in the tropics it produces reddish laterite soils—rich in iron oxides and aluminum hydroxide from the weathering of rocks. All around the world the land is nurtured, refreshed, and renewed in a continuing process.

Soil building helps to hold earth's biosphere together. It helps support creation's integrity by renewing the face of the earth. It is

yet another God-given provision, an expression of God's bountiful care for the world. If in 1923 Thomas Chisholm had wanted
to include this (and the next) provision in his famous hymn about
God's faithfulness, he might have written something like this:

> Summer and winter and springtime and harvest,
>> sun, moon, and stars in their courses above
> join with all nature in manifold witness
>> to thy great faithfulness, mercy, and love.
> Air and all elements, marvelously cycling,
>> tuned to the will of thy most loving grace,
> building earth's soils and supporting thy creatures
>> steeped in thy love across earth's wondrous
>>> face.

> —adapted from "Great Is Thy Faithfulness,"
> *Psalter Hymnal,* 1987, 1988; 556

3. Cycling and Recycling in the Biosphere

Recycling is not a recent invention. It is part and parcel of the
way the world works. The whole biosphere uses, reuses, and uses
again the various substances contained in soil, water, and air for
maintaining its living and nonliving fabric.

The Carbon Cycle. Carbon is the basic raw material from
which the carbon-based stuff of life is made. Even as you read this
book, you're contributing to the process of recycling this remarkable substance. As every living thing—whether human, raccoon,
lizard, or gnat—breathes out, carbon dioxide enters the atmosphere. This in turn is taken up by green plants to remake carbon
skeletons that give dynamic structure to all life. And this again is
transferred to animals and microscopic life that depend on carbon
for food—used both for building their carbon-based structure and
for meeting their energetic needs. And later they return this carbon
to the atmosphere as they again breathe out carbon dioxide or as
they die and decay.

The Hydrologic Cycle. Water too is cycled and recycled.

■ Taken up in the bodies of animals, water is released again
and again through breathing, sweating, panting, and waste
discharge. It then reenters the atmosphere, surface water, and
groundwater through natural means as well as through our
sewage treatment plants and septic tanks.

- Taken up by the roots of plants, water is pumped up through bundles of tubing in roots, stems, and leaves and is evaporated or transpired back into the atmosphere. Other water taken up by plants is used together with carbon dioxide to make the carbon-based stuff of life that, after use by plants and animals as building materials and fuels, is again returned to the atmosphere, surface water, and groundwater.

- The water that goes into the atmosphere—from plants, animals, and people—joins water evaporated from lakes, streams, soil, and other surfaces. This water eventually forms dew, rain, sleet, or snow that again waters the face of the earth. Some of this water is stored in packs of snow high in the mountains, or in glaciers great and small, that in time melt and supply water to streams and rivers below. Still other quantities of this water are stored in wetlands that will also in time slowly discharge it during times of drought. Other water from rain, sleet, or snow runs off to streams, rivers, and other surface waters ultimately to evaporate, again to form clouds. Some water percolates through the soil back to the roots of plants. Some slips past roots to enter the groundwater to be pumped by wells for human use or to emerge again as springs and eventually to return to the clouds from whence it came.

As water is evaporated or transpired to the air, almost everything that was dissolved in it is left behind. This sweet distillation expresses God's bountiful love for the world. And clouds—those great condensations of distilled watery vapors—rain down God's love again to water the earth in snow, dew, and rain. This cycle inspired the writing of Psalm 104:

> He makes springs pour water into the ravines;
>> it flows between the mountains.
> They give water to all the beasts of the field;
>> the wild donkeys quench their thirst.
> The birds of the air nest by the waters;
>> they sing among the branches.
> He waters the mountains from his upper chambers;
>> the earth is satisfied by the fruit of his work.
>> —Psalm 104:10-13

Cycles upon cycles . . . cycles within cycles . . . cycles of cycles—the creation is permeated with cycles. Each of these is empowered by energy poured out from the sun; each is held together by the power of God's Son (Col. 1:15-17).

The biosphere—the great envelope of life that embraces the face of the earth—is what we and all God's creatures inhabit. And all of it relies upon the cycles in creation. The biosphere consists of prairies, oceans, forests, lakes, glades, woodlands, brooks, and marshes. In other words, it is made up of wonderful and highly varied *ecosystems*.

Waubesa Marsh—the wetland on which I live—is one of these ecosystems. Like every other ecosystem on earth, this marsh has its plants, animals, soils, and climate:

- sandhill cranes whose six-foot wingspans, seventy-year lifespans, and bugling calls seemingly command the great marsh.
- iron bacteria whose smallness would escape our notice except for the oil-like film they create over quiet waters.
- deep peat soil at the edge of Lake Waubesa, soil that extends to a dizzying depth of 95 feet (29 m) and holds a record of pollens, seeds, and other remains that define its long history.
- the ebb and flow of water that comes in from rising groundwater, bubbling springs, and falling rain—and then leaves again by means of flowing streams, transpiration through the pores of wetland plants, and evaporation from the many surfaces of land, water, and living creatures.

All of these features and their interactions, and much more, make up the tapestry of this wetland ecosystem. Though it might not seem so at first glance—particularly for wetlands—ecosystems are places of immense ecological harmony. Not every feature plays the same "tune," but in many ways they are all "in tune" with each other and with the larger systems of which they are a part. Each ecosystem—wetland, forest, prairie, lake, and desert—is a kind of symphony.

The biggest ecosystem of them all—the biosphere—is like a symphony of symphonies. In relationship to each other, all plants and creatures and processes great and small contribute to the ecosystems of which they are a part, maintaining and sustaining the living structure of the biosphere. They continue to bring forth life from death as they cycle and recycle the basic stuff of creation, all powered by our star, the sun.

4. Water Purification and Detoxification

Taking a cue from nature, many water treatment plants in our cities purify water by filtering it through beds of sand in a process called *percolation*. Water that percolates naturally through the soil is purified in the same way, but usually over greater distances through soil and rock to the groundwater below. By the time it joins with groundwater that we can pump up to our homes from wells, this percolated water is usually fit to drink. This same purified water eventually also emerges from springs that feed wetlands, lakes, and streams.

As we have seen in the description of the hydrologic cycle, purified water is returned to the air by evaporation from the surfaces of water, land, and organisms, and from transpiration through the pores of leaves. We call this process *evapotranspiration*, or simply *ET*. ET from plants around the globe is essential for returning water to the atmosphere.

Flowing waters and their living inhabitants also serve as water purifiers. Normal levels of nutrients that enter streams from the land are processed by stream life. If not overloaded, this "ecosystem service" is another of God's important provisions that serves the biosphere well.

In addition, wetlands of many kinds across the globe act as water purification systems. Wetland plants filter out eroded soil carried by moving water and draw dissolved chemicals out of the water as they take up nutrients for growth. Mercury and other toxic heavy metals, for example, are taken up by wetlands and stored in the peat soils they form below. The result is that wetlands produce clear water for rivers and streams, thus keeping flowing waters and lakes habitable. Water clarity allows sunlight to reach aquatic plants, and water purification allows for fish and other aquatic life to flourish.

There is wonder in all of this! God remarkably provides for the production of pure water in nature. Contaminated again and again by sediments and dissolved substances, water is made pure again and again . . . and yet again!

5. *Fruitfulness and Abundant Life*

Creation is blessed with fruitfulness and abundant life! Life's home is the beautiful fabric of living things that envelops the entire earth—the wonderful fabric we call the biosphere. This fabric includes 250,000 species of flowering plants—orchids, grasses, daisies, maples, sedges, lilies—in amazingly colorful abundance and beauty. All of these interrelate with water, soil, air, and numerous organisms as they live interdependently and yet in their own distinctive ways. Beyond these are millions of other species of living creatures—all connected in a web of intricate dynamic interrelationships.

Millions of Fruitful Species. When I was in the ninth grade, I learned that there were about a million different kinds of living creatures. By the time I was in graduate school, I was taught that there were about 5 million species. Scientists today estimate that there may be up to 40 million species of living things on earth! The biodiversity of earth is so great that we are only just beginning to name its creatures. So far we have named only about 1.5 million species.

It is difficult to convey my utter amazement at the seemingly infinite variety of life on earth. I'm even more amazed that despite the dangers nearly every species faces as it goes through its life cycle, most species persist generation after generation, reproducing according to their kinds. Even in naturally occurring shifts in climate, landscape, forest cover, and other environmental surroundings, species persist from generation to generation because they can adapt to changing conditions. Each generation even has its own variety—hardly any two offspring are exactly alike. Such variety produces individuals that are endowed to adapt to new and unanticipated changes in their environment. God not only provides for each species to continue into future generations but also gives each one the blessed adaptability to flourish in new and changing situations. In other words, life not only persists—it flourishes.

Again we can turn to the psalmist to lead us in praise:

> How many are your works, LORD!
> In wisdom you made them all;
> the earth is full of your creatures.

There is the sea, vast and spacious,
    teeming with creatures beyond number—
    living things both large and small.

—Psalm 104:24-25

I remember vividly a reading of Genesis 1 by Atibisi, an African palynologist (palynology is the study of pollen found in wetland peat deposits). She sat on the floor with a group of us scientists and theologians in a meeting room in Malaysia prior to deliberations on the status of God's creation and our stewardship. She recited the first chapter of Genesis with awesome wonder and God-praising joy. This scientist, who used pollen profiles in layered peat deposits to unpack earth's record of seed plants going back to the earliest days of African agriculture, read the passage as an African storyteller. At the conclusion of her reading, this scientist proclaimed, "This is so true; never has there been written a more beautiful and truthful account of the coming of the biological diversity of our Lord's earth! 'Let the waters bring forth swarms of living creatures, and let birds fly above the earth across the expanse of the sky.' . . . And the Lord blessed them and said, 'Be fruitful and increase in number and fill the water in the seas, and let the birds increase on the earth'" (see Gen. 1:20, 22).

God causes the waters to bring forth swarms of creatures, and creation is blessed with fruitfulness. God's blessing is everywhere evident; it is awesome and wondrous!

Habitats. Although the Creator asked Noah to make special provisions and arrangements for the animals on Noah's ark (Gen. 6), that ship would not have been the best place for animals to live out their entire lives. Neither is a zoological park or a botanical garden! Thinking of Noah's ark and zoos and botanical gardens brings to mind the importance of habitats in the lives of earth's creatures. The ark needed someone like Noah, a zoo needs a zookeeper, and a botanical garden needs a gardener. But a natural habitat needs none of those—only the sustaining provision of the Lord. While human safeguarding and restoration of habitats can be helpful and necessary after human alteration or destruction, habitats are by nature self-sustaining and have existed in some form throughout the histories of the various species present with us on the earth today.

A habitat provides all the requirements needed by a living species to be fruitful and multiply. It allows a species to fulfill its role or "ecological niche" in the biosphere. Remarkably, with the great variety of ecosystems across the face of the earth and through the interrelations of geography, soils, climate, and living creatures, habitats are continuously being sustained and renewed. Often the actions of some species help produce the conditions required by other species. Added to this complexity is flexibility for the requirements of migrating animals. Shorebirds, for example, need a chain of favorable habitats along migration routes that for some species span ten thousand miles (16,000 km).

The distribution of living creatures and their habitats around the globe is the subject of *biogeography*. The biogeography of a given species is described by the size and geographic distribution of its supportive habitats. Variations in climate, soils, and many other factors produce biogeographic patterns and structure. Tundra habitats, for example, are found near the poles and high in mountains; deserts are often in the rain shadows of mountain ranges; and deciduous forests flourish in the mid-latitudes of the southern and northern hemispheres.

In their remarkable diversity, patterns, and supportive features, habitats are still another of God's bountiful provisions for life on earth. This provision—with its patterned structure, now so evident in satellite imagery of the earth—beautifully makes God's glories known.

The Fabric of Energy Relationships. Already we have briefly recognized that our star, the sun, energizes every green plant on earth and all creatures that eat them. The word *trophic* is from a Greek word that means "to nourish." Relationships that transfer nourishing energy from one species to another are called *trophic relationships*. These relationships are extremely important in the networking of living things across the entire world.

Green plants are at the first trophic level, meaning they get their energy directly from the sun. Other parts of God's creation—including us—receive energy indirectly from the sun by eating plants or by eating animals or other organisms that get their energy from plants. Rabbits are at trophic level 2 because they eat only plants. Bald eagles are at a higher trophic level because they eat fish that eat either plants or other things that eat plants. Everything that is not a green plant depends on eating living things for its energy. God's creatures produce and consume, multiply and diminish, develop and decompose, each depending directly or indirectly on the sun's light and each having a particular role in sustaining biospheric integrity.

Why must most plants be green? Because they contain green chlorophyll and are thus the only organisms on earth that can engage in the remarkable process of photosynthesis. Photosynthesis, the foundation of trophic relationships, is the means by which the sun's energy is captured by green plants for the benefit of all other living things on earth. Energy is the "currency" of creation's economy, and photosynthesis undergirds the trophic fabric that interlaces all of life.

A great provision by God, then, is (again) the sun. Another is photosynthesis, which converts solar energy into a form that plants and other creatures can use. Still another is the meshwork of trophic relationships that provide all earth's creatures the energy they need in order to live, reproduce, and flourish.

We—all creatures great and small—depend on these provisions for life. All of these are God's provisions—for which people pray and ravens call. "The lions roar for their prey and seek their food from God" (Ps. 104:21). And so God not only asks Job, "Where were you when I laid the earth's foundation?" but also inquires, "Do you hunt the prey for the lioness and satisfy the hunger of the lions . . . ? Who provides food for the raven when its young cry out to God . . . ?" (Job 38:4, 39, 41a). The answer is clear: God is their provider.

As we ponder these amazing discoveries in creation, our understanding of the symphonies of the biosphere grows. Along with the symphonies of trophic relationships and photosynthesis, there is even the symphony of "peculiar honors" each creature brings to creation's King.

> Jesus shall reign where'er the sun
> Does its successive journeys run;
> His kingdom stretch from shore to shore,
> Till moons shall wax and wane no more.
> Let every creature rise and bring
> Peculiar honors to our King,
> Angels descend with songs again
> And earth repeat the loud Amen.
> —Isaac Watts; *Psalter Hymnal,* 1959, 1976; 399

6. Global Circulations of Water and Air

Because of its 23½-degree tilt, our earth is unequally heated from season to season. The northern hemisphere gets far more solar radiation in summer than in winter. The opposite is true of the southern hemisphere. Besides these seasonal differences there are, of course, daily differences brought about by the rotation of the earth, which provides night and day, coolness and warmth, in a 24-hour cycle.

These seasonal and daily differences drive the flows of both water and air from place to place. Constraining and shaping these circulations, however, are land masses, ridges, valleys, and mountain ranges—both above and below sea level. The movements of water and air combine with all other symphonies in the biosphere to sustain life on earth.

As water and air circulate around the globe, they transport many different things such as carbon dioxide produced by animal and plant respiration, oxygen produced by photosynthesis, and water vapor breathed out by earth's creatures and evaporated from moist and wet surfaces. Carbon dioxide produced by animal and plant respiration is moved and mixed in the atmosphere in ways that bring it into contact with plants. Then plants take up this vital gas to use it in building the carbon backbone of all plant life and the animals that feed on it. Oxygen produced by photosynthesis is similarly circulated by air and water to supply vital respiration and energy conversion for animals and plants.

Global circulations are also vital movers of water vapor. The water put into the air by evaporation and transpiration rises to form clouds that in turn blow across land and sea to bring water to other places as rain, sleet, or snow. Global circulations are the ventilation system of the biosphere. Global circulations provide the "breath of life" on a planetary scale and are vital to the watering of God's great biosphere—the intricately interwoven fabric of life that envelops the earth.

If biblical psalmists had known of these global circulations and of creation's dependence on them, we might have had a psalm in our Bible that went something like this:

> You refresh the creatures with vital breath;
> you bathe your works in winds of life.

Your providence is everlasting.
Pastures green breathe life to flocks,
    to which your sheep return their wind.
Creation is securely held by your grace.
You ventilate the land and aerate your creatures.
    Your blowing renews the face of the earth.

7. Human Ability to Learn from Creation

God endowed human beings with the ability to learn from creation. The precious gift of being able to learn from the "beautiful book" of nature gives us the ability to observe, behold, investigate, and record in our mind's eye what we see, feel, hear, and smell. The images and ideas that then take shape in our minds help us plan and do our work in this world to the glory of our Creator. The learning we gain is also continually tested against our experience. We learn from our mistakes, learn from others whose observations and experiments we trust, and revise our models of the world to better represent the reality of the creation we live in.

This ability to learn from creation comes from God. A 1975 study of the *Hanunóo* tribe in the Philippine Islands, for example, found that an average adult from the tribe could identify 1,600 different species—all without the help of botanical science. These people had knowledge of some 400 more plant species than were previously recorded in a modern systematic botanical survey. What's more, they also knew how to use these plants for food, construction, crafts, and medicine. And they knew where to find all of them—they knew the plants' habitats and their ecology. Studies have produced similar findings in other areas of the world, such as Nigeria.[2]

The ability to build mental models and images of all aspects of creation—from atoms to plants to habitats to the cosmos—is essential for meaningful human life. These models are nurtured, transferred, and refined by our human culture, which is also a gift from God. Early in life we learned the warmth of our family's love, and we grew with love for our Creator as we learned about life in our community, school, and church family. We now con-

[2]Awa, N. "Participation and Indigenous Knowledge in Rural Development." *Knowledge* 10:304-316, 1989.

tinue enjoying these blessings daily as we also learn in our vocations and from the people and other communities around us.

Along the way we often are "re-minded" by people we meet and by places we visit. And in doing this, we may have to reevaluate what we hold in our minds to be true. We might even change our minds as we learn. In divine providence our minds are informed, cultured, and cultivated by learning from God's world and God's Word.

One way this can happen is by being "re-minded" that "the earth is the LORD's, and everything in it" (Ps. 24:1). Our minds may be cultured by the teachings of the Bible to learn of the One through whom all things were made, all things hold together, and all things are reconciled to God—as we read in Colossians 1:15-20. We might even follow biblical teachings that encourage us to be like-minded with Jesus Christ, who reconciles all creation to its Creator. Learning to adopt the mind of the Creator, Sustainer, and Reconciler is a joy and task that lasts a lifetime. Christian culture brings people to pray,

> May the mind of Christ, my Savior,
> live in me from day to day,
> by his love and power controlling
> all I do and say.
>
> —Kate B. Wilkinson; *Psalter Hymnal*, 1987; 291

What does it mean to adopt the mind of Christ, of whom it is written:

> The Son is the image of the invisible God, the firstborn over all creation. For in him all things were created: things in heaven and on earth, visible and invisible, whether thrones or powers or rulers or authorities; all things have been created through him and for him. He is before all things, and in him all things hold together. And he is the head of the body, the church; he is the beginning and the firstborn from among the dead, so that in everything he might have the supremacy. For God was pleased to have all his fullness dwell in him, and through him to reconcile to himself

37

all things, whether things on earth or things in heaven, by making peace through his blood, shed on the cross.

—Colossians 1:15-20

The Creator, in providing for all people, has given us minds and the capacity for mindful nurture of worldviews that allow us to image how the world works, to understand our place in it, and to act on our understanding in wisdom. We have been given the gift of being able to know God from his created world and from his Word, and to act on that knowledge to care for each other and for all creation. This provision allows us to adopt the mind of Christ, learning from the book of God's world and the book of God's works, to safeguard the integrity of creation and sustain and renew the life of the earth, in harmony with God's love for the world.

Suggestions for Group Session

GETTING STARTED

We can easily be distracted from considering closely God's provisions for us and for the rest of creation. Many people get so fully occupied on the treadmill of busyness that there is little time to reflect on God's amazing gifts. The air we breathe, the rain that waters the land, the new life that breaks forth from tiny seeds—often we take all of this for granted. We might never pause to think of the wheat plants whose fruit we enjoy every day, or of the remarkable beauty of the leaves we enjoy in our salads, or of why we never have to rake the leaves that fall in the forest. The greatest gifts are free. God pours out these gifts to each of us—and to all creation—every day and hour. This chapter celebrates these gifts.

Opening

If you are meeting as a group for the first time, I suggest that you begin by each mentioning a part of God's creation for which you are especially thankful. You might wish to include a recent experience in which you've particularly enjoyed some aspect of the creation, large or small. If your study of this is personal, you might want to pause and reflect on these things, and perhaps make an appropriate entry into your reflective journal (see Using this Book at the beginning of this volume).

Then you might enjoy reading these words from *Our World Belongs to God: A Contemporary Testimony* (para. 9):

> God formed sky, land, and sea;
> stars above, moon and sun,
> making a world of color, beauty, and variety—
> a fitting home for plants and animals, and us—
> a place to work and play,
> worship and wonder,
> love and laugh.
> God rested
> and gave us rest.
> In the beginning
> everything was very good.

You might then enjoy thanking God for these and other provisions in creation, giving praise, perhaps, to Jesus Christ, whom the Bible presents as the one through whom all things were created, hold together, and are reconciled to their Creator (Col. 1:15-20).

If you are discussing this chapter in a group, you may also wish to read Psalm 104 together.

FOR THOUGHT AND DISCUSSION

Here are some suggestions for a variety of activities you can do as an individual or in a group. You might not have time to do them all, so just choose the questions and activities that you think are most appropriate.

From this chapter

1. This chapter describes seven provisions that God has established for creation. Talk about one or two of these that impressed you most. Or maybe one of these provisions surprised or delighted you because you hadn't noticed it before, or had forgotten about it. What do these provisions tell us about creation? What do they tell us about God?

2. What other provisions has God given us in creation? Try to identify one or two more than the seven identified in this chapter. How many provisions do you think there are? Do you

think you could describe them all? Explain. (If you have time, you might tie this discussion in with a reading of some of the poetry in Job 38-41.)

From the Bible

3. Read Romans 1:20. What does this verse say about God's self-revelation in nature?

4. What does Colossians 1:16-17 say about God's continuing care for creation?

5. Read Psalm 19:1-6. What does this passage say about creation's response to God?

From your experience

6. How does God express love for the world? On a large sheet of paper, make a list of all the ways in which God shows love to the world. You may want to divide into small groups of three or four persons to come up with ideas. Think of the teachings of the Bible and about the evidence we see in creation of God's love for the world. Confine your list to the left half of your sheet of paper.

7. How might we image God's love for the world? On the right side of your paper, jot down ideas on how we can act to show God's love and care for creation. Try to pair each idea with a corresponding item in the left column.

PRAYER

In prayer you might wish to give thanks for God's creation, provisions, love, and care for the world. You could conclude with praise to God for Jesus Christ, God's one and only Son, our Savior, in whom all things hold together and are reconciled to God (Col. 1:15-20) and whose incarnation and resurrection give hope to the world.

02

Seven Degradations of Creation[1]

There was a time when I was oblivious to humanity's abuse of creation. I could always count on finding DeKay's snakes for my backyard zoo under tar paper and discarded sheet metal at the dump on the edge of town, and bullfrogs and bitterns were always present in the swamps surrounding Reeds Lake. I guess I just thought, as many of us do in our youth, that the world had somehow always been that way.

Many years later, however, while doing my graduate work with my wife, Ruth, on the desert of southern California, I became powerfully aware of the way human beings abused and were largely ignorant of creation. It was then that I first became embarrassed by the foolishness of our species. While I was studying the desert iguana—an abundant large, white lizard that lived in the dry, dusty land at the mouth of Deep Canyon—real-estate developers came to the foot of the San Jacinto Mountains with sprinklers to water the desert surface so it could be shaped with a blade, covered with a slab of concrete, and topped with a house. They were building on a great, gently sloping triangle of land, directing picture win-

[1]A full treatment of the provisions of the biosphere, in addition to a description of environmental abuses and needed response, can be found in Richard T. Wright and Bernard J. Nebel, *Environmental Science: Toward a Sustainable Future*, 10th edition (Englewood Cliffs, N.J.: Prentice-Hall, 2007).

dows of air-conditioned living rooms downslope to capture the magnificent view of the desert's grand sweep across the Coachella Valley.

What had formed the great triangle that sloped from the canyon's mouth and looked something like a river delta? The summer Ruth and I were there, it had rained only 2.54 inches (6.45 cm), normal for this dry area, so it clearly couldn't be a delta—or could it?

An old prospector who had wandered that desert for decades looking for gold explained: "Nope, it mainly never rains here. But when it does, watch out!" Pointing to the heights towering above us, he said, "Once a lifetime or so, up high in them mountains, it thunders and lightnin's, it rains cats and dogs. . . . Floods race down this canyon—spitting sand and rocks and boulders onto the desert below. That's what makes this delta here. Even boulders the size of houses come rollin' down in the ragin' river." Then lowering his arm and pointing to a protected point near the edge of the canyon, he said, "Over there, outside the path of the fury, is where the native people camped. They knew what this great delta meant!"

This site we selected for studying desert lizards would later become the city of Palm Desert, California. Seeds for this city were being planted right in the mouth of a giant river that once a century or so brought torrential floodwaters down from the Deep Canyon above!

Returning to the area in the 1990s, I found that what once was my study site had become the approach to a drive-in banking center along a major boulevard. What's more, as I spoke to the owners of the "Gates of the Desert Lodge," which had been sitting for decades in the former habitat of once-abundant white lizards, the proprietors looked bewildered when I asked about the "big white lizards." With puzzled expressions and bothered disbelief they replied to what seemed to them complete nonsense by saying, "Lizards?"

I was now standing in a city. The home of the hundred or so desert iguanas I had studied was now occupied by a drive-up bank. Nearby, cattails grew in a roadside ditch—wetland creatures were now thriving there in runoff from overwatered lawns. A fine mist descended from spray nozzles along the edge of a coffee shop awning. I did find one big white lizard nearby—at the local zoo. And whether they knew it or not, the people living on this great river delta at the mouth of Deep Canyon were waiting for the next great flood!

No longer am I ignorant of what people are doing in and to God's creation. And while I still sing, "Praise God . . . all creatures here below," it has become more of a hopeful doxology. I hope that God's big white lizards, God's deserts and prairies, and so much more will continue to exist and bring praise to their Maker. I hope that people discover the praise-giving of all creatures. I hope that people take care to learn well about their environmental surroundings so they can live more in harmony with creation, avoiding destruction of important habitats as well as avoiding danger for themselves and generations that follow.

What is the status of creation today? How are we faring as stewards of God's world? As people entrusted with the care of God's creation, we need to ask these questions, and they are not easy to answer. However, answering these questions has become part of my professional work. From an early computer search of 700,000 titles of articles on the environment, I selected those published in scientific, refereed literature and found that I could organize them into major topics that I call "Seven Degradations of Creation." That is the organization I will use in this summary.

Before proceeding with this summary, I must explain the meaning of "refereed literature." We know how referees are used in sports—they make sure the game is played by the rules. Similarly, refereed literature is read carefully by referees before it is published. Referees are carefully chosen for the depth and breadth of their knowledge and expertise, for their discernment and judgment, for their record of fairness, and for being free from the influence of sponsors and spectators.

The editors of refereed or "primary" literature normally use three referees to critically evaluate each article or "paper" (as professional research articles usually are called). For scientific literature, these referees are scientists who are peers of the scientist who is submitting a particular paper, have expertise in the particular field covered by the paper, and are not given the identity of the other two referees. After reading the paper, each of the three referees makes an independent, anonymous report to the editor and recommends whether to "reject," "publish," or "publish with revisions." If the editor gets a mixed review, the paper may be sent to still other qualified referees. If the paper must be revised, each revision is again reviewed by three referees in the same manner. Articles that pass these peer reviews are published periodically in professional journals, usually by a professional society of scientists to whom the editor is responsible. This highly disciplined procedure is designed to keep us researchers precise and thorough in reporting what we discover, in how we interpret our findings, and in how we place these in the context of advances in knowledge being made by other scientists in their refereed publications.

There are two other kinds of literature we should know about: "gray literature" and "popular literature." Gray literature consists of reports from government agencies such as state departments of natural resources, from colleges and universities, from granting agencies, and from think tanks, institutes, and foundations. This literature also is important, but it is not considered as authoritative because it does not undergo the same kind of disciplined peer review as does primary literature. Gray literature often uses different standards and is more susceptible to outside influences, and it may have items on its agenda that go beyond reporting new knowledge. As a result, it generally is not relied upon by professional researchers for a basic understanding of how the world works and what is happening to it. Popular literature consists of newspapers, magazines, leaflets, and brochures. Like gray literature, it also is important, and while it may be useful, it is not normally considered to be authoritative.

What I present here as "Seven Degradations of Creation" is based on primary or refereed literature. This means I have not gotten my information from government or university reports, newspapers, opinion polls, television talk shows, think tanks, or popular articles. This may mean that what I write about here on environmental degradation is less dramatic than what can be read or heard elsewhere, but it will not be boring. Instead, I'm sure you will find the topic of environmental degradation very interesting, and its magnitude often overwhelming! This chapter may in fact be so overwhelming that you might think things are hopeless. But that is not the case, as you will discover in later chapters.

SEVEN DEGRADATIONS OF CREATION
1. Alteration of Earth's Energy Exchange
In chapter 1, while thinking about how the biosphere relates to the rest of creation through the atmosphere—earth's great spherical envelope—we considered how energy flows through it, between

44

the earth and the sun, and between the earth and outer space. For a long time we simply took this remarkable gift for granted. While we did not understand very well its role in the rhythms of creation, we thought it to be so large that we couldn't change or degrade it. Somehow, it seemed, the atmosphere would always take care of itself and us, no matter what we did. We believed that it simply would continue to keep conditions favorable for life on earth.

Today, however, we have discovered that we cannot take the atmosphere for granted, the reason being that we are in the process of changing it. A basic requirement of good stewardship is to consider carefully whatever human beings affect, no matter how great or small. Good stewardship requires that each of us respond appropriately to the consequences of human action in the world, no matter how far our reach. And as our reach has now been extended even to the upper limits of the atmosphere, we must consider our impact upon it, particularly the adverse consequences for life on earth. Moreover, if we find we have an adverse impact, we will need to ask, "What must we then do?" as responsible stewards of creation.

Climate Change. Earth's atmosphere is a "crowning jewel" of the biosphere, which sustains life on earth and mediates energy flows between earth and the heavens. Much as many of us have not thought much about wetland ecosystems in the landscape, we also have not thought much about earth's atmosphere. Yet if we only pause to think of every smokestack, every chimney, and every automobile exhaust pipe around the world, each injecting chemicals and compounds into the atmosphere, we have good reason to think! If we then add thinking about still other ways by which we inject materials into the air around us, we have reason to think even more. Where does all of that "stuff" go? And what does all of that "stuff" do? The simple and immediate answer, not surprisingly, is that we are changing earth's atmosphere—both as the great radiation filter between earth and sun and as the system that processes and provides the air we and all other creatures breathe.

Beyond the many consequences of this injection to our lungs and breathing—such as asthma, emphysema, and lung cancer—consider how it may affect the "doorkeeper gases" we explored in chapter 1. "Greenhouse gases," as we have seen, are mainly transparent to visible light that comes from the sun through our atmosphere to the earth—but these gases are not transparent to infrared radiation emitting from the surface of the earth. We also know

45

that earth's atmosphere until recently had just the right amount of greenhouse gases to balance the amount of energy leaving earth with the energy coming to earth from the sun. We also know that our injections of chemicals and compounds have increased and continue to increase the amount of greenhouse gases in the atmosphere, including carbon dioxide, methane, chlorofluorocarbons (CFCs), hydrochlorofluorocarbons (HCFCs), and oxides of nitrogen (NO_x). These make our atmosphere more effective at retaining heat. And this greater effectiveness means that more energy is coming in through the atmosphere than goes out through the atmosphere. So what does this mean for earth's temperature?

Before dealing with that question, let's consider a very important part of this injection: the chemical element carbon and the oxide of this element, carbon dioxide. Carbon is an element that normally is in balance, with about the same amount being consumed by green plants in photosynthesis as is being produced by respiration and decay. This balance is indicated by the atmosphere having had about 250 to 300 parts per million over the past several thousands of years. The figure of 300 parts per million (by volume) is the basis for many of us having learned in school that carbon dioxide makes up about 0.03 percent of the gases in earth's atmosphere.

Now consider that we have been engaged in a large-scale burning of earth's deposits of carbon that were sequestered beneath us as peat, brown coal, soft coal, hard coal, and oil. Consider also the additional carbon that enters the atmosphere from widespread burning of forests and their carbon-based life and litter. Then consider what is less obvious but extremely important: additional carbon that is entering the atmosphere from the oxidation of carbon from soils around the world, brought about by removing vegetative cover and baring the soil surface to an oxidizing atmosphere, particularly by industrial agriculture. Carbon from all these sources is combined chemically with oxygen by oxidation, respiration, decomposition, and fire to become carbon dioxide. What is quite reasonable for us to expect with all of this is that the additional input of carbon dioxide into the atmosphere has come to be out of balance with carbon dioxide being removed from the atmosphere. That this is the case is indicated by the atmosphere now having an atmospheric carbon dioxide concentration of 380-390 parts per million, or about 0.04 percent of the atmosphere.

This means the concentration of atmospheric carbon dioxide has increased by about 33 percent (from .0003 to .0004) in less than one human lifetime.

What does that mean for earth's temperature? The answer should be clear, but I am not going to state it outright. Instead I am going to defer to the conclusions of a major chemical industry that has carefully researched the matter.

Before doing that, however, we need to recall that there are other greenhouse gases we have produced in the chemical industry and put into the atmosphere. And, more important, in a book seeking a biblical, Christian response to environmental issues, we must ask, "Who benefits from our not understanding this question or its answer? Who might be the ones working with such intensity and determination that many people in the United States, unlike the populations of many other nations in the world, consider the scientific findings about carbon dioxide and other greenhouse gases controversial?" The answer to the question "Who benefits?" is crucial to our seeking, finding, and knowing the truth.

Unlike in the case for ozone—our next topic below, regarding which there is a record of partnership between the chemical industry and policy makers—there is very little cooperation between the energy industry and policy makers. On climate change, as for ozone, it is in the immediate self-interest of industry either to be silent, to create doubt, to misrepresent the truth, or to create cynicism among the general public. And while the scientists in some chemical industries have been allowed to speak within their companies and to the public as scientists, this has not generally been the case for the energy industry.

Can we get an answer to our question on climate change from industry? The answer is yes. Here is one such answer: "We believe the scientific understanding of climate change is sufficient to compel prompt, effective actions to limit emissions of greenhouse gases. We believe that to be successful these actions will require concerted engagement by the world's governments, along with technological innovations by businesses, and individual actions by all citizens." This statement on climate change is that of a 200-year-old U.S. company that is setting aside some of its immediate self-interest to take concrete action to address climate change and to "urge action by everyone." It is one voice that detractors from the reality and urgency of climate change have not

47

been able to silence. It is the voice of E. I. du Pont de Nemours and Company, known more commonly as DuPont.

As I think and reflect personally on this from my Christian perspective on life and truth, I find that we are confronting a degradation even more serious than adverse climate change. It is a degradation of information and understanding, fueled by false witness, intentional misrepresentation, and calculated deception of the U.S. populace. False witness, deception, misrepresentation, and general dishonesty are frequently addressed in Scripture and judged seriously as sin. This sin of deception has been so effective that many U.S. citizens have been led not only to deny what can be seen with our own eyes, but also to be willing to discredit DuPont and the honest assessment of climate change by their scientists. One of DuPont's leading climate scientists, Dr. Mack McFarland, participated in Climate Forum 2002, a gathering that Sir John T. Houghton and I convened in Oxford, England, to bring leading climate scientists and evangelical leaders together. That forum's call for action, the Oxford Declaration on Climate Change, is included after this chapter as an "Interlude" (see p. 61) and is well worth our thoughtful consideration.

Depletion of the Ozone Shield. Earth's ozone shield, as we noted in chapter 1, absorbs much of the sun's ultraviolet radiation, protecting life from damage to its DNA. However, ozone destruction has been under way particularly through the production of chlorofluorocarbons (CFCs) that were once widely used as refrigerants, fire-extinguisher ingredients, hair-spray propellants, blowing gas for foam plastic manufacture, and more. These gases, including the one once marketed by DuPont as Freon, eventually ended up in the high atmosphere, where they were found to destroy ozone. Destruction of the ozone shield by CFCs—now being addressed but in need of careful monitoring—results in more ultraviolet light reaching earth. Ultraviolet rays kill microscopic creatures on earth and cause skin cancer in people and animals. Thankfully many policy makers and businesses and chemical industry executives today have recognized this serious problem, and in an agreement called the Montreal Protocol on Substances that Deplete the Ozone Layer they have begun implementing a program for protecting the ozone shield and are meeting with success. Hydrochlorofluorocarbons (HCFCs) and hydrofluorocarbons (HFCs), developed to be used in place of CFCs, have themselves been discovered to be a problem because, like CFCs, they are also potent greenhouse gases, being up to 10,000 times more powerful than carbon dioxide as a greenhouse gas. Here too there are bright rays of hope, thanks to the Montreal Protocol and cooperative work with the chemical industry, with plans and actions well on the way to phase out the production of these chemicals, with a 90 percent reduction planned by 2015, 99.5 percent by 2020, and 100 percent by 2030.

2. Soil and Land Degradation

During the latter half of the twentieth century, nearly one-third of arable lands worldwide were lost to erosion and taken out of production. In Asia, Africa, and South America annual soil loss was about 14 tons per acre, and in the United States and Europe the loss was about 7 tons per acre—all of which contrasts sharply with annual soil formation rates averaging about 0.4 tons per acre. And the losses are compounded by associated reductions of water infiltration, soil water-holding capacity, topsoil thickness, soil carbon sequestration, organic matter and nutrients, soil biota, and productivity; by associated increases of water runoff, surface water eutrophication, and siltation of rivers and streams; and by reduction of hydroelectric capacity by siltation of reservoirs (D. Pimentel, et al., 1995), which were lost to erosion and taken out of production.

Pesticides and herbicides, produced after military chemists shifted their attention to developing "peaceful" uses of biocides after World War II, made it possible to plant corn, or any crop, year after year on the same land. Crop rotation—from corn to soybeans to alfalfa hay, for example—and pasturing and fallowing were largely abandoned in North America. Farmers became "free" to plant the same crop year after year—and often were urged to do so by chemical manufacturers and their salespeople. This allowed farm animals to be kept in feedlots and confinements that allowed for intensified use of the land. Topsoil lost by resulting wind and water erosion could be compensated for by increasing fertilizer inputs. As a result, soil life has been devastated.

Earthworm populations have either been killed off in most land used for industrial agriculture, or in some cases earthworms have flourished but have become toxic and thus problematic for the rest of the food chain. The microscopic life of the soil has been severely altered. Fencerows and hedgerows have largely been removed, reducing habitat for farmland birds. Most of the land never rests. Much land has been converted into chemical desert. Even many domestic creatures no longer have pastures or pastors. Thoughtfulness is necessary here, including application of Scripture, as with any other degradation. An example: "When you enter the land I am going to give you," says the Lord, "the land itself must observe a sabbath to the LORD" (Lev. 25:2). A related example is God's warning to Moses that if the people did not obey this law, the land would be laid waste. After the land had become a desert, the people would be driven away. Then the land would have the rest it did not have while the people lived on it (Lev. 26:14-17, 32-35). Perhaps some might say, "That Scripture was for ancient times. It does not apply to us now." But does it?

3. Consumption, Waste, and Ecosystem Dysfunction

In our day, 80,000 different chemicals are being used in commercial quantities, most of them brand-new to earth's biosphere, with about 1,000 more being added each year. Many and perhaps most of these are part of the environment in which we and other organisms live. Yet these are materials that living organisms have not had experience with in the past. Unlike chemicals made by organisms and the earth, some of these chemicals leave living things defenseless. Some are even specifically designed to destroy life: biocides, pesticides, herbicides, avicides, and fungicides. Other materials pose additional problems for living things. For example, oil spills destroy life and habitats and devastate human livelihoods on shores and seas. Mercury from smokestacks rains down on the earth and its creatures.

Every item in our homes, offices, churches, and industries is a reworked part of creation. Every product we make, each housing and commercial development we build, every road we travel alters creation. While knowing this full well, we often neglect to recognize the immense changes that we billions of people bring to the earth. We remove parts of the creation, make products and by-products, and produce discards and wastes.

Consider styrofoam cups as an example. We move oil by ship from Saudi Arabia to chemical plants. There the oil is transformed into *monomers*, which are then transported to factories that mold them into styrofoam cups. These cups are distributed to stores, where we buy them for use in our homes, schools, and churches. After using them once, we discard them into wastebaskets, move them to trash containers, and truck them to landfills. As the cups slowly decompose, their remains liquefy to form leachate, which is either drained off and processed by a sewage plant or leaks into groundwater that may next contaminate springs and wells. As styrofoam decomposes, it also produces carbon dioxide, methane, and other materials that add to greenhouse gases in the atmosphere. We often justify their use because they are more convenient than using reusable ceramic cups.

Ours is mainly a flow-through economy. It taps creation's wealth at one point and discards by-products and wastes at another. By contrast, nature's economy is cyclical; ecosystems sustain themselves by cycling materials. Our economy threatens creation's economy. We interfere with nature's cycles on a grand scale as we "trash" its creatures, pollute its waters, and mow down its forests and prairies.

As we consider this degradation, we should thoughtfully reflect on this passage from Ezekiel: "Is it not enough for you to feed on the good pasture? Must you also trample the rest of your pasture with your feet? Is it not enough for you to drink clear water? Must you also muddy the rest with your feet?" (Ezek. 34:18).

4. Land Conversion and Habitat Destruction

Since 1850 people have converted 2.2 billion acres of natural lands for human uses (8.9 million square km, an area slightly smaller than China's total land area of 9.2 million square km). Compare this with earth's 16 billion acres that support some kind of vegetation (a nearly equal area consists of ice, snow, and rock) and a current world cropland of 3.6 billion acres. The conversion of land goes by different names, depending on what is done: it may be called deforestation (forests), drainage or "reclamation" (wetlands), irrigation (arid and semi-arid ecosystems), or opening (grasslands and prairies). The greatest land conversion under way today is tropical deforestation, which removes about 25 million acres of primary forest each year—an area the size of the state of Indiana.

The immensity of this destruction illustrates humanity's power to alter the face of the earth. Why do we continue with tropical deforestation? Largely because we are *able* to—and because it allows us to make inexpensive products like cheap plywood, bathroom tissue, and packaging for all kinds of things from orange juice to fast-food hamburger meals. All this comes at the cost of destroying the long-term sustainability of soils, forest creatures, and resident people.

In the United States and Canada, woodlots and the habitats they provide are replaced with parking lots, buildings, and additions to homes, offices, and churches. Of the 400 million acres of cropland in the United States, about 2 million acres are converted to urban uses every year.

The Bible speaks to this particular degradation when it says, "Woe to you who add house to house and join field to field till no space is left and you live alone in the land" (Isa. 5:8).

5. Species Extinctions

There are some 10,000 known bird species, of which about one goes extinct each year. (One scientist calls this vanishing of whole species "the death of birth.") If action is not taken to preserve birds, 12 percent of all known bird species are predicted to become extinct by 2099. In sizing up the status of creation, a worldwide coordinated effort by scientists produced the Millennium Ecosystem Assessment, stating that if needed action is not taken, 23 percent of mammals, 25 percent of conifers (pines, spruces, and their relatives), and 32 percent of amphibians will be threatened with extinction during this century.

Sylvia Earle, a scientist who leads Conservation International's Global Marine Division, adds the following comment on worldwide industrial fishing: "With 70 percent of the world's coastal fish stocks overexploited or collapsed and 90 percent of the biggest fish wiped out, we have turned to the deep oceans in our increasingly relentless and destructive pursuit of the dwindling supply of seafood." One indication of this is that for our Friday-night fish fries (popular in some regions), the fish no longer come from Cape Cod but from Iceland.

While we have given names to most species of plants and animals in North America and Europe, we have not completed the work of naming the species in the tropics. Named or not, however, many of those species appear in our stores, lumber yards, offices, boats, and homes in the form of cheap plywood, furniture, wallets, and shoes. Children around the world are paid pennies to bring in skins of once-living creatures that are manufactured into fashion items.

We add to this species destruction when we destroy natural habitats by expanding our homes and churches and eliminating woodlots or wetlands. Even butterflies, once so common in the everyday life of city and country, are losing hold as their habitats are destroyed, their food plants are killed by herbicides, and they themselves are killed by "broad-spectrum" pesticides.

Some ecologists now urge us to plant butterfly gardens as natural "arks" for preserving these creatures. Others urge preservation of remaining woodlots and prairies as natural "arks" in response to what has become a "deluge of people and pavement." Even now, some churchyards in England, because they remain largely undisturbed by real-estate development, are the sole remaining habitats for some creatures.

A Scripture verse to ponder as we consider these losses is Genesis 6:19, in which the Lord says to Noah: "You are to bring into the ark two of all living creatures, male and female, to keep them alive with you."

6. Global Toxification

A major feature of the earth's dynamic weather, ocean, and river systems is their life-sustaining transport and distribution of materials around the globe. Of the thousands of chemical substances people have created, hundreds have been injected into the atmosphere, discharged into rivers and oceans, and leaked into groundwater by means of "disposal" systems and by pollution from our vehicles, homes, chemical agriculture, and industry. Some have joined global circulations, with substances like DDT showing up in Antarctic penguins and biocides appearing in a remote lake on Lake Superior's Isle Royale. Cancer has become pervasive in some herring gull populations and is increasingly prevalent in our communities and congregations. Chemical and oil spills kill creation's life on a massive scale. Globally circulating toxins disrupt ecosystems, and hormone-mimicking chemicals create reproductive disorders and affect normal development in animals and people.

In the interaction between creation's economy and ours, we face a planetary challenge: the consequences of what some call "the rape of the earth." No longer are *local* environments affected only by *local* polluters. Global toxification affects all life: all creatures, great and small; all people, rich and poor. Our earth is precious; it proclaims God's glory! But it is not being treated

53

with love and care; it has become for many people in our day a mere bag of resources, even a trash bag to receive the things we throw "away." In creation, of course, there is no "away." Every square inch belongs to its Maker, and it is to our Maker that we are responsible stewards.

We need to reflect on the words of Jeremiah 2:7 as we consider what we human beings have done to God's creation: "I brought you into a fertile land to eat its fruit and rich produce," says the Lord. "But you came and defiled my land and made my inheritance detestable."

7. Human and Cultural Abuse

Among the most severe reductions of creation's richness is degradation and extinction of cultures that have lived peaceably and sustainably on the land for centuries. Many Amish and Mennonite farming communities in North America, for example, operate under severe pressure from increasing land taxes and encroaching urban development. In many cases these pressures compel them to abandon their farms. In the tropics, longstanding cultures living cooperatively with the forest are being wiped off the land by force, death, and legal procedures devised to deprive them of their traditional lands. As these people are run off or extinguished, so is their rich heritage of unwritten knowledge. Successful ways of living in harmony with the land are forgotten, names of otherwise undescribed forest creatures are lost, and information on the uses of a wide array of tropical species for human food, fiber, and medicine is wasted.

Agri*culture* is being displaced by agri*business*. Seeds of a wide variety of plants suited to small farms and gardens are displaced by new strains suited to industrial planting and harvesting—strains uniform in color, size, and time of ripening. An aggressive human economy, seeking to maximize immediate return at the expense of long-term sustainability, is sweeping the globe. The meek people of the earth are displaced by labor-saving technology; the powerless are pushed to the margins of the land or into cities. Disconnected from land that could sustain them, they are driven into joblessness and poverty. In the name of conducting "good" business and making "sound" investments, power brokers deprive powerless people of the ability to take care of themselves and the creation.

Where farmers and agrarian culture remain in the world—and they number about 2.5 billion people, all of whose livelihoods are in farming—stewardship of land held in trust over the generations generally remains the cultural and ethical norm. But external factors increasingly push these people to the margins, even eliminating them and their agrarian culture altogether. Agrarian culture is degraded and destroyed, and soil stewardship is maintained only to the extent that it is required for present and immediate gains. Local knowledge and local investment in land and soil are discarded. As a result, the pleasure of living on the land, the wholesomeness of agrarian culture, and the beauty of the earth are diminished. A June 5, 2008, article in the *New York Times* titled "Food Is Gold, So Billions Invested in Farming" illustrates this transformation of land from trust to commodity: "Huge investment funds have already poured hundreds of billions of dollars into booming financial markets for commodities like wheat, corn, and soybeans. But a few big private investors are starting to make bolder and longer-term bets that the world's need for food will greatly increase—by buying farmland, fertilizer, grain elevators, and shipping equipment. . . . And three institutional investors . . . are separately planning to invest hundreds of millions of dollars in agriculture, chiefly farmland, from sub-Saharan Africa to the English countryside." The article explained that a major firm planned "to consolidate small plots into more productive holdings" in Africa, primarily because "land values are very, very inexpensive" there. Food becomes money, land becomes commodity, and "investors" are distanced from the land and from the people who are engaged in its life for their everyday living.

God's Word says, "Do not take advantage of each other. . . . The land must not be sold permanently, because the land is mine and you reside in my land" (Lev. 25:17, 23). The Bible also says that the land must be returned to the poor and meek (Lev. 25:28). The Lord observes that "even the stork in the sky knows her appointed seasons, and the dove, the swift and the thrush observe the time of their migration. But my people do not know the requirements of the LORD" (Jer. 8:7).

CHOOSING LIFE

Creation's garden abundantly yields blessed fruits, sustainably supporting us and all life in its God-declared goodness. But the descendants of the first Adam have made the choice to extract more and yet more at the expense of destroying creation's protective provisions and blessed fruitfulness. Before this human onslaught fall earth's creatures. Some are severely diminished; others are wiped off the face of the Creator's canvas. We often find ourselves living at a time when many have chosen to trash the great gallery of earth's Maker, replacing it with their own creations. These new creations claim to be "for the greatest good" and "bigger than life"— surpassing creation itself. Under this arrogant assault on the fabric of the biosphere "the earth dries up and withers. . . . The earth is defiled by its people" (Isa. 24:4-5).

Since the beginning of creation, human beings have been making choices. Early on, we chose to know good and evil (Gen. 2:15-17; 3:1-7). In the past several centuries many have chosen to redefine the long-recognized vices of avarice and greed as virtues. We have come to believe that "looking out for number one" means getting more and more for ourselves. *Self*-interest, we now profess, is what brings the greatest good. Choices made for the creation, for the Creator, have been usurped by choices made for *me* and "the economy." Our world professes, "Seek first a job (money, success), and all other things will be yours as well" (compare to Matt. 6:33). The biblical view, by contrast, calls us to find our "vocation" in God's creation.

God says through Moses, "I have set before you life and death, blessings and curses. Now choose life, so that you and your children may live and that you may love the LORD your God, listen to his voice, and hold fast to him. For the LORD is your life . . ." (Deut. 30:19-20).

While we are expected to enjoy God's creation and its fruitfulness, we are not granted license to destroy the earth. While human beings are expected to be fruitful, so is the rest of creation: "God said, 'Let the water teem with living creatures, and let birds fly above the earth and across the vault of the sky.' . . . God blessed them and said, 'Be fruitful and increase in number and fill the water in the seas, and let the birds increase on the earth.' . . . 'Let the land produce living creatures according to their kinds, creatures that move along the ground, and wild animals, each according to its kind.' And it was so" (Gen. 1:20-24). Our expansion may not be at the expense of the fruitfulness of the rest of creation.

Suggestions for Study

GETTING STARTED

It is easy to go about living without ever thinking about the results of our actions. We frequently throw things "away," never thinking about where "away" is. We spray a substance designed to kill an insect, never wondering whether that substance will kill or hurt other life as well. We decry the destruction of the great trees of California as we chat around our redwood picnic table. We are part of a society that has distanced us from the results of its actions. And the result of all this is that the creation is being degraded. This chapter describes some of the major degradations of creation and helps build an understanding of why we need to be concerned for creation and for future generations.

Opening Prayer

You might wish to begin by praising God for the marvelous provisions given in creation, and then confessing our participation in degrading God's creation, knowingly and unknowingly, by action and inaction. You might then wish to ask God for forgiveness and for the grace to engage in reconciling action that results from repentance.

Scripture Readings

As a group, look up and read the following passages in the order in which they are listed here. What beauties and provisions of creation do these Scriptures describe? In what ways are people called to account for their actions?

Genesis 1:1-5

Jeremiah 4:23

Genesis 1:20-22

Jeremiah 4:25-26

Leviticus 26:27, 32-35

Ezekiel 34:18-19

FOR THOUGHT AND DISCUSSION

How do we connect with these degradations of creation?

1. On the left side of a large sheet of paper make a list of the seven degradations of creation noted in this chapter. Then, on the right side of the page, write down how we personally contribute to each of these degradations in our daily lives.

What can we learn by reflecting on our childhood?

2. Think back to something that in your childhood or early youth was a wonderful part of creation but now has been degraded or destroyed. Describe it and what happened to it. Or reflect on whether the climate was different back then, and describe your observations.

What do we know about the things we buy and where they come from in creation?

3. Identify one item you have purchased in the past week and sketch out or describe on a piece of paper where it originated, how it eventually came to you, and where it ultimately is going. Then discuss the following questions:

   - How far has it traveled?
   - What effects has this item had on creation in the course of its journey?
   - What information is provided on the label or other information that came with this item?

Can we read natural signs of changing weather and climate?

4. Read Matthew 16:2-3 and Luke 12:54-56. Use these passages as a starting point for asking if we are able to interpret the signs of changing weather and climate, and proceed to discuss our understanding of these.

What are the underlying causes of environmental abuse?

5. Invite group members to suggest what they think is the greatest environmental abuse we are facing in today's world. (Various answers may be given.) Then, all together or in small groups of three or four, identify the underlying cause or causes of *all* the abuses you have identified. (If people divide into small groups, have a reporter from each group share its findings with the larger group.) Discuss the main cause or causes of

degradation to God's creation and what must be done about it. What does society have to say about it? What does the Bible say? Is addressing this important? Why or why not?

Isn't saving people more important than saving species?
6. Sometimes Christians ask, "Isn't it more important to save people than to save species?" Invite group members to share their initial thoughts. Then refresh yourselves on the story of Noah and the flood in Genesis 6-9. You might reflect by asking questions like these:

   ■ Why did God save living creatures, according to their kinds (species), as well as people?
   ■ If saving people always is more important than saving species, how might this story have been written?

7. Read John 3:16 and Revelation 11:18. What do these passages tell us about God's love and care for the world as well as its people?

What can I do?
8. Select one of the seven degradations we have studied in this chapter and describe what we can do about it in our personal lives and our community.

Do we and society know the meaning of sin?
9. Douglas John Hall in his book *Imaging God: Dominion as Stewardship* points out that some environmental scientists today who study environmental degradation are helping us rediscover the meaning of sin—and these scientists are not necessarily Christian.

   ■ What do you think—has our society lost a sense of the meaning of sin?
   ■ Have Christians lost a sense of the meaning of sin? If so, in what way? If not, why not?
   ■ How would you describe humanity's abuses of creation to a person who might not know God?

PRAYER

While preparing to close in prayer, consider what you have learned about the underlying cause or causes of environmental degradation and what to do about it. Think through the importance of confession and repentance in connection with abuses of God's creation. In doing this, remember that repentance means more than saying we are sorry for what we have done and left undone; it also includes responding with appropriate actions. If you are with others, you may wish to conclude with a confessional prayer in which everyone is welcome to participate.

Oxford Declaration on Climate Change
Climate Scientists and Christian Leaders Call for Action

I n an unprecedented forum of climate scientists and evangelical Christian leaders convened at Oxford, England, in 2002, there emerged, through the development of a scientific and Christian understanding of the world by means of presentations and discussions, a keen perception of the need to call upon leaders in churches, business, and government to join in recognizing human-induced climate change as a moral and religious issue and to take necessary action to maintain earth's climate system—a system that is a remarkable provision in creation for sustaining all life on earth. This is Climate Forum 2002's statement to the world. (See www.jri.org.uk/news/statement.htm.)

Human-induced climate change is a moral, ethical, and religious issue.

- God created the Earth and continues to sustain it. Made in God's image, human beings are to care for people and all creation as God cares for them. The call to "love the Lord your God . . . and . . . love your neighbor" (Matthew 22:37–39) takes on new implications in the face of present and projected climate change. God has demonstrated his commitment to creation in the incarnation and resurrection of Jesus Christ. Christ, who "reconciles all things" (Colossians 1:20), calls his followers to the "ministry of reconciliation" (2 Corinthians 5:18-19).

- Human-induced climate change poses a great threat to the common good, especially to the poor, the vulnerable, and future generations.
- By reducing the Earth's biological diversity, human-induced climate change diminishes God's creation.

Human-induced climate change, therefore, is a matter of urgent and profound concern.

The Earth's climate is changing, with adverse effects on people, communities, and ecosystems.

- There is now high confidence in the scientific evidence of human influence on climate as detailed by the Intergovernmental Panel on Climate Change (IPCC) and endorsed by 18 of the world's leading Academies of Science.
- Human activities, especially the burning of coal, oil, and natural gas (fossil fuels) are rapidly increasing the concentrations of greenhouse gases (especially carbon dioxide) in the global atmosphere. As a result the global climate is warming, with rising sea levels, changes in rainfall patterns, more floods and droughts, and more intense storms. These have serious social, economic, and ecological consequences.
- The harmful effects of climate change far outweigh the beneficial ones.
  - In many arid and semi-arid areas, the quantity and the quality of fresh water will continue to decrease.
  - Although agricultural productivity may increase in temperate northern latitudes, it will decrease throughout the tropics and subtropics.
  - A greater incidence of diseases, such as malaria, dengue fever, and cholera, is expected.
  - Sea-level rise and increased flooding are already displacing people and will eventually affect tens of millions, especially in low-income countries. Some island states are likely to disappear altogether.
  - Important ecosystems, such as coral reefs and forests, will be destroyed or drastically altered, undermining the very foundation of a sustainable world.

Action is needed now, both to arrest climate change and to adapt to its effects.

■ We must take immediate steps to stabilize the climate. This means reducing global emissions of carbon dioxide to below 1990 levels well before the middle of the 21st century.

■ While industrialized nations have largely caused the problem, its most severe effects fall upon the peoples of developing countries. Industrialized countries need therefore to make much greater reductions in emissions in order to allow for economic growth in developing countries.

• We urge industrialized nations to take the lead in reducing their emissions. They have the technical, financial, and institutional ability to do so now.

• We urge industrialized countries to assist developing countries in gaining access to cleaner and renewable forms of energy.

• We urge that actions be taken to increase energy efficiency in transportation, buildings, and industry. Many actions can produce savings or be taken at little or no net cost. Examples were presented to the Forum of such actions by 38 major multinational companies.

• We urge greater use and development of renewable sources of energy.

• We urge increased financial investment and that banking initiatives be grasped to enable the necessary changes.

■ The cost of inaction will be greater than the cost of appropriate action.

■ Adapting to the impacts of climate change (e.g., droughts and flooding) is not an alternative to mitigation but is essential, given that the climate is already changing and further change is inevitable.

Christian denominations, churches, and organizations need to take action to

■ increase awareness of the facts of global climate change and its moral implications;

■ set an example through individual and collective actions that reduce greenhouse gas emissions;

■ increase demand for technologies and products that produce fewer emissions of carbon dioxide;

- urge immediate and responsible action by national governments, in cooperation with other governments under the Framework Convention on Climate Change. This should be, first, to ensure the successful operation of the Kyoto Protocol (which some countries, including the United States, Canada, and Australia, have not yet ratified) and, second, to establish an effective programme of emissions reductions in the period immediately following that covered by that Protocol.

We, the forum participants, recognize the urgency for addressing human-induced climate change, repent of our inaction, and commit ourselves to work diligently and creatively to adopt solutions in our own lives and in the communities we influence. We call upon leaders in churches, business, and government to join us in recognizing human-induced climate change as a moral and religious issue and to take necessary action to maintain the climate system as a remarkable provision in creation for sustaining all life on Earth.

Chairs and Key Speakers

Dr. John Biggs, Environmental Issues Network of Churches Together in Britain and Ireland; Steering Committee, Eco-Congregation, UK

Dr. James Bruce, former Head of Atmospheric Environment Service, Canada; former Co-chair of IPCC Working Group 3

Prof. R. J. (Sam) Berry, Professor of Genetics, University College London, UK

Rev. Richard Cizik, Vice President for Government Affairs, National Association of Evangelicals, USA

Mr. Henry Derwent, Department of Environment, Food and Rural Affairs, UK Government

Prof. Calvin DeWitt, Au Sable Institute and University of Wisconsin-Madison, USA

Prof. James Drummond, Department of Physics, University of Toronto, Canada

Ms. Nafia D'Souza, Director, Laya, India

Dr. Job Ebenezer, former Head of Environmental Stewardship Office, ELCA, Chicago, USA

Dr. Jae Edmonds, Chief Scientist, Pacific Northwest National Labs, Joint Global Research Institute, USA

Rt. Hon. John Gummer, M.P., former Secretary of State for the Environment, UK

Prof. Michael Grubb, Professor of Climate Change and Energy Policy, Imperial College, London, UK

Sir John T. Houghton, former Co-chairman of Scientific Assessment Working Group, IPCC; Chairman of The John Ray Initiative, UK

Rt. Rev. James Jones, Bishop of Liverpool, UK

Rev. Dr. Ernest Lucas, Vice-Principal and Tutor in Biblical Studies, Bristol Baptist College, UK

Dr. Mack McFarland, Principal Scientist, Environmental Program, DuPont, USA

Prof. Jesse N. K. Mugambi, University of Nairobi, Kenya

Dr. John Mitchell, Meteorological Office, Hadley Centre for Climate Prediction and Research, UK

Rev. John Paarlberg, Minister for Social Witness and Worship, Reformed Church in America, USA

Dr. Rafe Pomerance, Chairman, Board of Directors, Americans for Equitable Climate Solutions, USA

Dr. Robert Watson, Director Environment, World Bank, Washington, D.C., USA, and former Chair of IPCC

interlude two

Buying Back Time

I n December 2010 I was an official observer at COP 16—officially known as the United Nations' 16th session of the Conference of the Parties—focusing on climate talks in Cancun, Mexico. There I heard a fine presentation by Mexico's Nobel laureate, Mario Molina, who, along with his professor at the University of California-Berkeley, Sherwood "Sherry" Rowland, discovered how CFCs were destroying the ozone layer in earth's stratosphere. (CFCs were being widely used as refrigerants, fire retardants, blowing agents for foam plastics manufacture, and aerosol sprays.) Molina was speaking on a panel of other experts on Near-Term Climate Change Mitigation. The important point he made was that action on CFCs had been pretty straightforward: the scientific case was made on the mechanism for stratospheric ozone destruction by CFCs, policy deliberations took place based upon the scientific case, and thereafter followed in 1989 the worldwide adoption of the Montreal Protocol on Substances that Deplete the Ozone Layer. The Montreal Protocol has been immensely successful in dramatically reducing and nearly eliminating industrial production of CFCs. However, as Molina's fellow panelist, the distinguished chemist Veerabhadran "Ram" Ramanathan, told us, he reported in 1975 that CFCs are extremely powerful greenhouse gases that can be thousands of times more powerful than carbon dioxide. I found it remarkable that both Molina and Ram were in the same room together, telling us not only of their discoveries but also translating these into public policy.

As he sat at the table in front of us, Ram asked himself, "Why am I here?" He replied by saying, "Because we have lost time! But, more than that, I am here also to say that we can *buy back time.* We can buy back time by getting at these gases that I and others have discovered to be powerful greenhouse gases!"

The power of what Molina and Ram were telling us soon sank in to the audience. We had achieved a near-term partial solution to climate change by reducing and eliminating gases that—while in much smaller concentrations than carbon dioxide—were so many thousand times more potent that their elimination would have nearly immediate and profound effects. Another of the panelists, Achim Steiner, executive director of the United Nations Environment Programme, reflecting on what we have been learning about stratospheric chemistry, observed that for too long we have treated science as a luxury—something that informs us about our planet and our place on earth. But, he said, "We are moving now from . . . science as something that *allows* us to act, to science that *requires* us to act. We are moving from nature study to necessary action."

So it was of great interest a couple of days later to pass by the U.S. Center at COP 16 and be handed a sheet describing a meeting that was about to begin. Sponsored by the U.S. Department of State and the U.S Environmental Protection Agency, it reported on trilateral work by the U.S., Mexico, and Canada to address hydrofluorocarbons (HFCs). Panelists reviewed how we had met with great success in eliminating CFC production so that it would no longer be added to the stratosphere, where it would further increase the ongoing destruction of the protective ozone shield of our planet. But they also summarized how replacement of CFCs with HFCs, while eliminating ozone-depleting chemicals, failed to address these chemicals as greenhouse gases. The HFCs turned out also to be potent, and even more potent, greenhouse gases. The panel concluded that the Montreal Protocol—as an extremely successful approach to eliminating CFCs—should now be extended to eliminate HFCs and other similar greenhouse gases.

The session was on a World Wide Webcast, and questions after the presentations came from as far away as India. As I caught the eye of the man with the microphone, he allowed me to question the panel: "What are the prospects for using carbon dioxide as a replacement for HFCs, in refrigeration, for example? And what are the disincentives that might be present to prevent this from happening? And how might these disincentives be removed?" The answer to my question was affirming: "Already there are 50 stores in Australia that have converted over to carbon dioxide refrigerants; many vending machines also use carbon dioxide, as do some refrigerated produce shelves in supermarkets. As these examples come to be known, this use of carbon dioxide could become extremely widespread."

"Well!" I thought. "Another commercial use for carbon dioxide? And, more, a use of carbon dioxide that would replace the thousands-of-times-more-powerful CFCs, HFCs, and more? Wonderful, it seems to me!"

While I reflected on these encouraging thoughts, the person in front of me turned to give me his card, affirming my enthusiasm for the use of carbon dioxide as a refrigerant. His card identified him as Didier Coulomb, Director, International Institute of Refrigeration. And from his website I read this: "Sainsbury's has doubled the size of its supermarket in Durham, UK, and has cut energy consumption by 10 percent. The store will be 'carbon negative,' thanks to a number or technologies including groundbreaking CO_2 refrigeration technology and on-site renewable power generation. The energy efficiency features and renewable energy generation will enable the carbon footprint of the store to be neutralized within a mere two years. This is the first Sainsbury's extension to use CO_2 refrigeration, and the chain's CEO has announced the company's intention to switch to CO_2 refrigeration in all stores by 2030. By 2019, new legislation is expected to ensure that all new commercial developments in the UK will have to be zero carbon." Inspiring!

03

A Biblical Perspective on Creation Care

We know that over the centuries the Bible has been critically important to people who seek to live in love and obedience to God. The Bible's importance continues today, not only for church and home but also (and this surprises many Christians and non-Christians alike) for the environment. The Bible is hardly a minor contributor on caring for creation. In fact, the Bible provides such powerful environmental teachings that it can be thought of as a kind of ecological handbook on how to live in harmony with the earth!

Among its many teachings the Bible helps us understand our privilege and responsibility for environmental stewardship—for creation care. The Bible also helps us thoughtfully address who we are, how we have failed to live up to our God-given identity, and what problems we have made for God's creation.

The Bible's serious treatment of environmental matters should not surprise us. Since God creates and sustains all of creation, we should expect the Bible to call us to bring honor to God in creation. We should expect Scripture to support creation's care and keeping and to encourage us to maintain the integrity of the creation that God repeatedly calls "good" (Gen. 1:4, 10, 12, 18, 21, 25, 31). Moreover, since the Bible professes Jesus Christ as the one through whom *all things* are reconciled to God (Col. 1:20), we should expect it to decry creation's destruction, to call for creation's restoration, and to look forward to the whole creation's being made right again. And so it does!

Keeping in mind the degradations we have summarized and being aware that many people today yearn to restore the integrity of creation, it can be helpful to read the Scriptures afresh, searching for their ecological insights on how to live in harmony with creation and to share the joy of such living. The following sections of this chapter identify eight biblical principles that help disclose the Bible's powerful environmental message. No doubt you will be able to identify many other biblical principles as well.

1 THE EARTHKEEPING PRINCIPLE

As the Lord keeps and sustains us, so we must keep and sustain our Lord's creation.

Genesis 2:15 conveys a marvelous teaching. Adam is expected by God to *serve* the garden and to *keep* it.

The Hebrew word for *serve* (*'abad*) is translated as "till," "dress," and "work" in some recent versions of the Bible. But "serve" is also a possible translation, as in *Young's Literal Translation of the Bible*. God expected Adam and his descendants to meet the needs of the garden of creation so that it would persist and flourish. But how can we *serve* creation today? This certainly is a puzzle we can discuss with our friends. (We'll talk more about this when we discuss "The Con-Servancy Principle" later in this chapter.)

God also expected Adam and Adam's descendants to *keep* the garden—to be responsible "guardeners." The word for *keep* (*shamar*) is sometimes translated as "guard," "safeguard," "take care of," and "look after." *Shamar* indicates a loving, caring, sustaining kind of keeping.

In our worship services, we often conclude with the blessing from Numbers 6:24: "The LORD bless you and keep you. . . ." In the original Hebrew text, the word here for "keep" is *shamar*. When we invoke God's blessing to *keep* us, we are not asking that God would keep us in a kind of preserved, inactive state. Instead, we are calling on God to keep us in all of our vitality, with all our energy and beauty. The keeping we expect of God when we invoke this ancient blessing is one that nurtures all of our life-sustaining and life-fulfilling relationships—with family, neighbors, and friends; with the land, air, and water of the earth; and of course with God.

So too with our keeping of God's creation. Our relationship to creation must be a loving, caring, keeping relationship. When we fulfill God's mandate to *keep* the creation, we make sure that the creatures and other living things under our care are maintained so that they can flourish. They must remain connected with members of the same species, with the many other species with which they interact, and with the soil, air, and water they depend on.

As God *keeps* believing people, so God's people should *keep* his creation.

2 THE FRUITFULNESS PRINCIPLE

We should enjoy but not destroy creation's fruitfulness.

God's blessing of fruitfulness is for the whole creation. In Genesis 1, God declares, "Let the water teem with living creatures, and let birds fly above the earth across the vault of the sky" (1:20). And God blesses these creatures with fruitfulness: "Be fruitful and increase in number and fill the water in the seas, and let the birds increase on the earth" (1:22). God also says, "Let the land produce living creatures according to their kinds, creatures that move along the ground, and wild animals, each according to its kind" (1:24).

God's creation reflects God's fruitful work, giving to land and life what satisfies and sustains it. Psalm 104:10-13 expresses this beautifully:

> He makes springs pour water into the ravines;
>   it flows between the mountains.
> They give water to all the beasts of the field;
>   the wild donkeys quench their thirst.
> The birds of the air nest by the waters;
>   they sing among the branches.
> He waters the mountains from his upper chambers;
>   the land is satisfied by the fruit of his work.

In addition, Psalm 23:2-3 describes how our providing God gives us rest "in green pastures," leads us "beside quiet waters," and "refreshes" our souls.

As God's fruitful work brings fruit to creation, so should ours. As God provides for all his creatures, so should we who are created to reflect God's image. As Noah cared for God's creatures when they were threatened with extinction, so should we. In Noah's time a flood of water covered the land. In our time floods of people in many places sprawl across the land, often displacing God's other creatures, limiting *their* potential to fulfill their blessing and God's command to be fruitful. To those who would allow a human flood across the land at the expense of all other creatures, the prophet Isaiah warns, "Woe to you who add house to house and join field to field till no space is left and you live alone in the land" (Isa. 5:8).

So while we are expected to enjoy creation and its many fruits, we may not destroy the *fruitfulness* that creation's fullness depends on. Like Noah, we must preserve and care for God's many species whose interactions and relationships with each other and with land and water make up the fabric of the biosphere. We must let the profound admonition of Ezekiel 34:18 echo in our minds: "Is it not enough for you to feed on the good pasture? Must you also trample the rest of your pasture with your feet? Is it not enough for you to drink clear water? Must you also muddy the rest with your feet?"

3 THE SABBATH PRINCIPLE
We must provide for creation's sabbath rests.

In Exodus 20 and Deuteronomy 5, God commands us to set aside one day in seven as a day of rest for people and for animals. This sabbath day is given to help us all get off "the treadmill," to protect us all from the hazards of continuous work, to help us pull our lives together again. It's a time to worship the Lord and enjoy the fruits of his creation, a time for rest and restoration. In Exodus 23:12, God commands, "Six days do your work, but on the seventh day do not work, so that your ox and your donkey may rest, and so that the slave born in your household and the foreigner living among you may be refreshed."

The same chapter in Scripture says that the land also must have its time of sabbath rest. Nothing in all creation must be relentlessly pressed. "For six years you are to sow your fields and harvest the crops, but during the seventh year let the land lie unplowed and unused. Then the poor among your people may get food from it, and the wild animals may eat what they leave. Do the same with your vineyard and your olive grove" (Ex. 23:10-11).

Does this command create a problem for people? Leviticus 25:20-21 says, "You may ask, 'What will we eat in the seventh year if we do not plant or harvest our crops?'" God's answer: "I will send you such a blessing in the sixth year that the land will yield enough for three years." God was instructing people not to worry but to practice his law so that the land would be *fruitful*. "If you follow my decrees and are careful to obey my commands, I will send you rain in its season, and the ground will yield its crops and the trees their fruit" (Lev. 26:3-4).

In the New Testament, Jesus clearly defines for us the meaning of sabbath in our lives: the sabbath is made for those who are served by it—not the other way around (Mark 2:27). The sabbath is made for people and, through them, for all the rest of God's creation. The sabbath year is given to protect the land from relentless exploitation, to help it rejuvenate, to give it a time of rest and restoration.

This sabbath is not merely a legalistic requirement; it's a profound principle. That's why in some farming communities the land is allowed to rest every *second* year, because that is what it needs. The sabbath is made for the land—not the land for the sabbath. The sabbath law is therefore not restricted to agriculture but applies to all of creation. It affects our use of water and air, for example, as we discharge our exhaust, smoke, sewage, and other things we "throw away." God speaks strongly on this issue:

> "If you will not listen to me and carry out all these commands, and if you reject my decrees and abhor my laws . . . and so violate my covenant . . . your land will be laid waste, and your cities will lie in ruins. Then the land will enjoy its sabbath years all the time it lies desolate . . . then the land will rest and enjoy its sabbaths. All the time that it lies desolate, the land will have the rest it did not have during the sabbaths you lived in it."
>
> —Leviticus 26:14-15, 33-35

These are harsh words from the holy Creator who is concerned for his creation. But God's promises of blessing are equally powerful for all who will listen:

> "If you keep your feet from breaking the Sabbath
> and from doing as you please . . . then you will
> find joy in the LORD, and I will cause you to ride
> in triumph on the heights of the land. . . ."
>
> —Isaiah 58:13-14

4 THE DISCIPLESHIP PRINCIPLE

We must be disciples of Jesus Christ—the Creator, Sustainer, and Reconciler of all things.

No question about it—the Bible calls us to be disciples, or *followers after* someone. But we are not to be disciples of the Adam of Genesis, who neglected to serve (*'abad*) and keep (*shamar*) the creation. We must not follow those who choose to go their own way and do their own thing.

Instead, the Bible tells us, we must be disciples of the *final Adam*, Jesus Christ (see 1 Cor. 15:45). In John 3:16 the New Testament teaches that God loved the world so much that he gave his only Son—to bring true life, to make things right again. "For as in Adam all die, so in Christ all will be made alive" (1 Cor. 15:22).

All who follow Jesus follow the example of the one who makes all things new, the one who makes all things right again (Rev. 21:5). Colossians 1:19-20 puts it this way: "God was pleased to have all his fullness dwell in him, and through him to reconcile to himself *all things*."

Who is this Christ we are to follow? He is the one *in whom* and *for whom* all things were created (Col. 1:16). He is the one *through whom* God made the universe and *through whom* God redeems his people (John 1:3; Col. 1:16, 20; Heb. 1:3).

God reaches out sacrificially to make things right again. Jesus Christ, the final Adam, undoes the damage done by the first Adam and his followers. While followers of Adam bring death and degradation, Christ brings life and restoration (Rom. 5:12-17). The children of God work as followers and disciples of the final Adam. People who are happy being Christ's servant stewards are people for whom the whole creation is eagerly looking (Rom. 8:19).

We must, then, be disciples of Jesus Christ. We walk in the footsteps of the one who reconciles all things. We walk the path of the one who takes the form of a reconciling servant. As disciples of the last Adam, we work to reconcile all things to God in Christ.

5 THE KINGDOM PRIORITY PRINCIPLE

We must seek first the kingdom of God.

Our culture today proclaims, "Seek first a job (money, success), and all other things will be yours as well." It is tempting to yield to this message and to follow people whose highest priority is to gather up immense material gains. But Jesus advises us to seek first the kingdom of God and God's way of doing things; then everything else we need will be given to us as well (Matt. 6:33).

Personal happiness, joy, and fulfillment are not what we seek first of all in life. Instead we seek the kingdom of God and strive to sustain and renew God's creation. In seeking God's kingdom, we discover that happiness and joy are *by-products* of our stewardship; fulfillment comes as a *result* of seeking the kingdom.

Who will inherit this kingdom? Believers who seek it as their first priority. Its inheritance is not for people who arrogantly exploit their neighbors, the land, and earth's creatures for all they are worth. Nor is the inheritance for those who carelessly and knowingly destroy the earth.

Seeking God's kingdom first is our calling, our vocation. We affirm this calling whenever we pray as Jesus taught us: "Our Father in heaven, hallowed be your name, your kingdom come, your will be done, *on earth . . .*" (Matt. 6:9-10).

6 THE CONTENTMENT PRINCIPLE

We must seek true contentment.

The fruitful and beautiful creation did not satisfy our first parents and succeeding generations. Even though God promised not to forsake or leave them, people chose to go their own way— grasping more and more from the creation for selfish advancement. In our day we feel the effects of this relentless pressing of land and life to produce more—ever more. This relentless pressing is what is so seriously degrading God's creation today. Everyone's prayer today should be that of Psalm 119:36: "Turn my heart toward your statutes and not toward selfish gain."

If accumulating the goods of creation is selfish gain, then what is godly gain? Godly gain is doing the work God would have us do in the world. In 1 Timothy 6:6 we learn that "godliness with contentment is great gain." Contentment means aiming to have the things that will sustain us while not pressing beyond that. An Amish saying based on this passage goes like this: "To desire to be rich is to desire to have more than what we need to be content."

Why is it important not to pass the point of contentment? In the words of 1 Timothy 6:11, by not passing this point we can "pursue righteousness, godliness, faith, love, endurance and gentleness." Hebrews 13:5 puts it this way: "Keep your lives free from the love of money and be content with what you have, because God has said, 'Never will I leave you; never will I forsake you.'"

Being content helps us personally, and it helps preserve creation's integrity. All the things we use, all the things we make, everything we manipulate, everything we accumulate derives from creation itself. If we learn to seek godly contentment as our great gain, we will take and shape less of God's earth. We will demand less from the land. We will leave room for God's other creatures. We will be responsible stewards, caretakers, keepers of creation. We will regularly allow creation to heal itself and perpetuate its fruitfulness, to the glory and praise of its Maker.

7 THE PRAXIS PRINCIPLE
We must practice what we believe.

The Scriptures admonish us to act on what we know is right. Merely knowing God's requirements for stewardship is not enough. Merely believing in God is not enough, for Scripture tells us that even demons believe in God (James 2:19). We must practice God's requirements, or they do no good.

More than this, the Scriptures admonish us to seek and discern the truth. When we seek the truth, in accord with John 8:32, we find that the truth includes the teachings of Jesus Christ. When we see the enemy coming, we must sound the alarm (Ezek. 33). When we are commissioned to save God's creatures, we must be responsive and faithful (Gen. 6-9). And when we are tempted to misrepresent the truth, we must resist, bearing true witness to what is right, by proclaiming and doing it (Ex. 20:16; Prov. 12:15-20; Matt. 4:1-11).

The failure of people to act on what they know is right is well-documented—and challenged—in the pages of Scripture:

> "My people come to you, as they usually do, and sit before you to hear your words, but they do not put them into practice. Their mouths speak of love, but their hearts are greedy for unjust gain. Indeed, to them you are nothing more than one who sings love songs with a beautiful voice and plays an instrument well, for they hear your words, but they do not put them into practice."
>
> —Ezekiel 33:31-32

> "Why do you call me, 'Lord, Lord,' and do not do what I say?"
>
> —Luke 6:46

Christian environmental stewardship does not end with the last chapter of a book such as *Earthwise*. Instead, reading this book and studying the Bible to learn God's requirements for creation care marks a beginning point. It brings us directly to the question *Now what must we do?* The challenge before us is to move forward and put what we know and believe into practice.

8 THE CON-SERVANCY PRINCIPLE

We must return creation's service to us with service of our own.

This principle overarches all the others. The word *conservancy*, as you may know, refers to conservation and often denotes an organization that regulates fisheries and/or protects other natural resources. In this discussion I hyphenate this word to draw attention to its root meaning—*con + serve* means "to serve with."

You remember that, as we considered the earthkeeping principle, we noted from Genesis 2:15 that Adam and Adam's descendants were expected to be "guardeners," responsible caretakers commissioned to *serve* the garden and to *keep* it. The Hebrew word *'abad* ("serve") in this passage occurs 290 times in the Old Testament, and it is most often translated as "serve," as in Joshua 24:15: "Choose for yourselves this day whom you will serve. . . . As for me and my household, we will serve the LORD."

The various Bible translations of *'abad* in Genesis 2:15—
"serve," "till," "dress," and "work"—relate to worthy service. God
calls us to give the garden of creation our caring service.

We already know from experience with the "beautiful book"
of creation that this garden serves us. It serves us with good food,
beauty, herbs, fiber, medicine, pleasant microclimates, continual
soil-making, nutrient processing, and seed production. The garden
and the larger biosphere provide what ecologists call "ecosystem
services" such as water purification by evaporation and percolation, moderation of flood peaks and drought flows by river-system
wetlands, development of soils from the weathering of rocks, and
moderation of local climates by nearby bodies of water. Yet Genesis addresses *our* service to the garden. The garden's service *to us*
is implicit; service *from us* to the garden is explicit.

Like Adam and Adam's descendants, we are expected to return
the service of the garden with service of our own. This is a reciprocal service, a "service with"—in other words, a *con-service*, a
con-servancy, a *con-servation*. This reciprocal service defines an
engaging relationship between garden and gardener, between the
biosphere and its safeguarding stewards.

So we can call this "never taking from creation without returning service of our own" the *Con-Servancy Principle* (or *Con-
Servation Principle*). Our love of our Creator God, God's love of
the creation, and our imaging this love of God—all join together
to commission us as *con-servers* of creation. As *con-servers*, we
follow the example of the final Adam—Jesus Christ (see 1 Cor.
15:22, 45).

Suggestions for Study

GETTING STARTED

We don't usually think of the Bible as a kind of handbook on how
to care for God's creation. But in part that's what it is. The Bible
has much to teach us about living in harmony with God, with
other people, and with all of creation. We know that the Bible's
teaching is done in the context of knowing and celebrating God
as Creator and Sustainer of all things. So we really can expect the
Bible to inform us on living harmoniously in God's creation—and
so it does. In this chapter we open ourselves and our minds to

the Bible's teachings on caring for the earth entrusted to us—on "serving with" the earth to honor and praise the Lord, our Maker and Savior.

Scripture Readings
Genesis 1:26-28; 2:15

John 1:1-5; 3:16-21

Colossians 1:15-20

Revelation 11:15-18

Opening Prayer
You might like to begin by thanking God for the beauty of creation, for the testimony it gives of God's everlasting power and divinity, and for God's testimony in the Bible. You might also want to express appreciation that God has not left us without guidance. As you praise God for showing his love and care for creation, consider praying that we—imaging God—may also love and care for creation, and that in our world today we may take very seriously the teachings of Scripture, specifically noting biblical teachings on earthkeeping, fruitfulness, and sabbath. And, of course, *con-service!*

FOR THOUGHT AND DISCUSSION
What are some good texts for framing?
1. Suppose you were asked to select three Bible passages about caring for creation so that they could be reproduced on wall plaques. Which ones would you choose?

Are biblical teachings about creation relevant today?
2. Write out the passage from Ezekiel 34:18 about the muddying of water and the trampling of pastureland.
   ■ Is this passage relevant to the degradation of water and land today? Explain.
   ■ Does this passage tell us anything about how we should treat the rest of creation? Why or why not?

3. What does Isaiah 5:8 say to us about the way we use land today?

4. What are some ways we can provide for creation's "sabbath rest"? (See Ex. 23:10-11.)

5. Share your thoughts on the relationship between Genesis 1:26-28 and Genesis 2:15. How do these two passages help to explain each other? What do they tell us about our relationship to God and our relationship to God's creation?

What's your stewardship rating?

6. On a scale of 1 (poor) to 10 (excellent), how would you rate your personal stewardship of God's creation? Share your rating and the reasons for it with others in the group, and discuss ways in which you could help each other as you strive to do God's will in caring for creation.

PRAYER

The Bible is a rich source of wisdom, and its depth becomes more and more evident as we "turn it about," thinking deeply about what it has to teach us.

As you close, you might thank God together for the Bible, for its depth of meaning, and for what it brings to our lives as we work to live in obedience and love for our Lord. You might also pray specifically for the Spirit's encouragement and empowerment to act on what you've learned here about earthkeeping, fruitfulness, sabbath rest for creation, and serving with the creation to honor God. Let me suggest that you finish by reading aloud the ancient blessing found in Numbers 6:24-26.

May the Lord bless and *keep* you!

Note: The next session requires a careful, reflective reading. You'll want to set aside extra time to thoughtfully consider what it says as it lays out a theological foundation for understanding how we should serve as individuals and as the church in and with God's creation.

04

A Theological Perspective on Creation Care

The principles of *Earthkeeping, Fruitfulness,* and *Sabbath* join with the principles of *Discipleship, Kingdom Priority, Contentment,* and *Praxis* to inform and guide creation care. Embraced by the overarching principle of *Con-Servancy,* they lie at the heart of environmental stewardship, extending from tiny ecosystems to the whole of earth's biosphere.

Because gardens and gardening are also a part of creation, these principles apply to them as well. It is, after all, in a garden—the Garden of Eden—that the Bible introduces us to responsible care for creation. So it is fruitful for us to begin this chapter by focusing on gardens and gardening as we work to discover more fully the meaning of stewardship. It also is fitting to begin where we left off in the previous chapter—with the Con-Servancy Principle.

From the text that gives us the Con-Servancy Principle (Gen. 2:15) we learn that Adam and Adam's descendants were expected to return the service of the garden with service of their own. God's intent in this *relationship* is that both the gardeners and the garden would flourish and be fruitful. This relationship of reciprocal service is vital to responsive gardening and is the key to garden stewardship, as every successful gardener knows. This back-and-forth sustaining relationship is similar to the kind of service that engages us with the biosphere—engages us as players in the great symphony of life that envelops our earth. And, wonderfully, what we discover from our relationship with the garden and the biosphere is that they have a lot to teach us.

The garden, with its many leafy and floral species, with its colorful and life-perpetuating fruitfulness, helps us see how we gain knowledge by "reading" the things God has made. It teaches us how to expand on this knowledge by learning from others who delight in gardening—from neighbors and relatives, master gardeners, field naturalists, ecologists, climatologists, soil scientists, and other amateurs and professionals. These people too gain their knowledge by reading the creation and by reading things from others who also read creation's "beautiful book." Their delight brings them to study things great and small, and their learning comes to us in the form of lectures, gardening manuals, field guides, recordings, magazines, books, videos, and television specials—and as refereed papers that receive careful scrutiny and affirmation by full-time students of creation.

GARDENERS AND STEWARDS

As we investigate gardening and stewardship, a good way to begin is to think about caring for a "house plant" in a flower pot. By our "back-and-forth" relationship with it, we learn what our plant needs to survive and flourish. As we shift its location and give it nutrients and water, it teaches us its needs—for fertile soil, sunlight, water, the right temperatures, and more. It responds to our care with growth and color and beauty—with its "song" of praise to the Creator of life. When light is available, it also produces some of the oxygen we need (by way of photosynthesis) in return for using some of the carbon dioxide we breathe out—another essential provision from our Creator.

Moving to our garden outside, we find that it teaches us more. There we learn how we bring ourselves to provide for the needs of individual species and the garden as a whole. As gardeners, we are shaped and molded as caretakers in accord with what the garden and our gardening tell us it needs to flourish and be fruitful. We serve the garden's needs and enjoyment, even as it serves ours.

Being stewards of God's wider creation—the biosphere—is much like that. We learn directly about the biosphere by our own observations and study, and we learn indirectly from others. We learn what is needed to bring ourselves into harmony with the requirements for sustaining the biosphere. The essence of creation stewardship involves adjusting to and acting in accord with creation's need to sustain itself and to flourish with abundant life. In return, creation provides the habitat for us in which we also can enjoy flourishing, abundant life.

During the process of learning from the biosphere, our delight increases. More than that, our awareness and respect for it and its creatures increase. As we learn more, we are inspired to live in harmony with creation and to learn even more. And, when the biosphere and its supportive provisions for us and other life are threatened, we work to safeguard its flourishing and abundant life.

Pause at this point to reread the epigraph at the beginning of this book, written in 1554 by John Calvin. Then read it again, exploring your thoughts that come to mind in light of our "back-and-forth" relationship with God's creation. Note Calvin's saying that Adam was given custody of the garden, meaning that Adam was commissioned to be a gardener. Is it remarkable that Calvin could express these thoughts hundreds of years ago? Why or why not?

Now, just as there are great differences between a flower in a pot and the many interactive species in a garden, there are great differences between a garden and the entire creation! One truly amazing difference is that there are vast parts of creation that need no help from us. We don't have to draw up water to form the clouds, produce the thunder and lightning of great storms, give orders to the morning, or govern earth's climate system. Neither do we have to guide and arrange the constellations of the heavens, cause the eagle to soar, construct a fully functioning hippopotamus, or call forth earth's vegetation to cover a new lava field. Nor do we have to direct earth's living creatures to live in harmony with their habitats, find food, reproduce, and otherwise flourish. God provides for and takes care of all these things—and much more!

So we are not gardeners of the entire creation. We are not even gardeners of the biosphere. But we are its stewards! At the very least we are stewards of everything in the biosphere on which our human life and society have an impact. And since our impact today has become global, it is increasingly necessary to know that we are called to be stewards of the entire earth. This also makes it necessary for us to explore together what our stewardship of the biosphere means—practically, ethically, and theologically.

BAG OF RESOURCES? OR BEAUTIFUL BOOK?

From the Scriptures we know that ever since the creation of human beings, God has been in an interactive *relationship* with us. Ever since God breathed into us the breath of life and impressed upon us his image, God has been with us, and we have belonged to our Maker. More than that, God made us his imagebearers so that we might reflect and image his love and care for the world and thus bring glory and honor to him. People have often affirmed and celebrated this relationship—in which the Lord promises to be our God and we promise to honor God as his people. The covenant of circumcision was one of the earliest examples of this mutual relationship (see Gen. 17:1-8). Then about two thousand years later the sign and seal of baptism affirmed this relationship for New Testament believers in Christ, who fulfilled all the requirements of the earlier covenant, reconciling us with God, opening the way for us to be saved from sin so that we may live with God forever.

History shows all too clearly, however, that we have broken our promises to God again and again. Early on, when humankind was young, we pressed beyond the boundaries of the garden God gave us. As a result, we came to know (to experience) evil as well as good (Gen. 2:16-17; 3:11). And this pressing has continued through the millennia so that creation's testimony to God's glory, divinity, and eternal power is now often obscured (see Ps. 19:1; Rom. 1:18-23). Our pressing has gone so far that we have even come to look on creation as a kind of "bag of resources" in contrast to thinking of God's creation as a "beautiful book," as we noted earlier. Moreover, the wonder of God's provisions—for example, everyday photosynthesis—is now mainly taken for granted. Worse yet, God's provisions are now often regarded as mere mechanisms that we sometimes even think we can "improve." In many ways this kind of thinking and acting has overtaken us and brought the whole creation into a kind of suffering and groaning (Rom. 8:20-21).

As I think of the "beautiful book" metaphor, I am reminded of a great library. We can think of any of the world's great libraries as a great treasure house of recorded learning and knowledge. Imagine, though, that we come upon a library without understanding or caring about reading its texts. Imagine that we might not even know that the printed characters in its books make up words and sentences. Suppose also that—not recognizing these as stores of knowledge—we view these books as fuel, nicely packaged and arranged in neat stacks for us to use in our wood-burning stoves! (Author and scholar Thomas Cahill tells us in his book *How the Irish Saved Civilization* that people in ages past have actually viewed books this way!)

This illustration hits home for me in the great marsh just outside my back door. This peatland on which I live is itself a history book. Beneath its surface are preserved, layer by layer, yearly records of its own past. Each of its annually deposited layers contains pollen grains that fell from wetland plants or blew in from surrounding hillsides. The layers also contain seeds and snail shells left from the life that flourished here thousands of years ago and into the present. Remarkably, some of these layers also contain volcanic ash. Whenever great volcanic eruptions in the distant past gave off ash that blew around the globe, some of it dropped into my peatland, and the ash now resides in different layers that mark various years and centuries.

I have learned, with my graduate students, to read this ash and pollen. From pollen, for example, we discover that in its early years the marsh was surrounded by a spruce and fir forest; then later it became part of an open prairie in what is now southern Wisconsin. From the volcanic ash we learn something about the timing and intensity of the blowup of Mount Mazama—the eruption that created Crater Lake in southwestern Oregon. Winds from the western coast of North America carried its ash along and deposited it here about 5,700 years before the time of Jesus Christ.

Yet, remarkable and unique as creation's great history books are as sources of knowledge, large tracts of their "sodden pages," entire volumes, and whole libraries are being destroyed elsewhere. Some peat volumes are dried and burned in stoves to heat homes on Irish moors, some are ground up to provide sphagnum mulch for gardens, and some are drained and left to decompose into water and carbon dioxide by exposure to atmospheric oxygen. In a sense, we really *do* burn up and ruin storehouses of valuable knowledge today—not because we do not appreciate information and knowledge, but because we do not appreciate or even recognize the language in which these volumes are written.

Thanks to the work of leaders in conservation efforts, however—perhaps most notably a hundred years ago in North America by U.S. president Theodore Roosevelt—there are hundreds of preserves on our continent today in the form of national forests, bird sanctuaries, protected wetlands, and national parks. These efforts have also been modeled around the world to safeguard pages and chapters of the "beautiful book" of creation.

As I have worked with colleagues, particularly in the effort to discover "The Root Causes of Unsustainability" in creation at a consultation and writers' workshop at Cambridge University in England, I have come to understand that much of our industrial world today views creation more as a bag than as a book. Along with this shift in the way we view the world—a shift in our worldview—my university students, in seeking to find the underlying causes of environmental degradation, have concluded that it has nothing to do with the way the world works but with the way human beings behave in the world—by human arrogance, ignorance, and greed, something the students labeled "AIG" a few decades ago. In my work with professional colleagues at the Cambridge meeting, I also found the root of environmental degradation to reside in institutional corruption and decay—a degradation driven in large part by arrogance, ignorance, and greed. This is part of a diagnosis of our unsustainable condition in creation.

So you might now have an inkling why this book is titled *Earthwise*. "What the world needs now," as an old song says, "is love . . ."—including love for God and God's creation. We need a love so intensive and extensive that it extends to transforming ourselves, our churches, our communities, and our institutions to become "earthwise."

Finding that being "dollar-wise and earth-foolish" does not provide the way toward a renewed and vibrant creation, we must seek to restore and sustain the integrity of creation—the integrity of God's kingdom for whose coming we pray—". . . on earth . . ." (Matt. 6:10).

STEWARDSHIP IN OUR DIFFERENT PLACES

As we appreciate creation and read and learn from the pages of this elegant book, we do so in the places we live—across the continent and around the globe. Our places of living and doing include countrysides, towns, villages, and cities. The regions where we live feature all kinds of ecosystems, including tropical forests, boreal forests, prairies and steppes, mountains, deserts, wetlands, oceans, and more. Our stewardship is defined and shaped by the places we live and by our local ecosystems. And whatever our stewardship is locally, it will join with a regional and global stewardship, informed by other stewards around the globe.

What this means is that our stewardship is rich and full. Our stewardship of the biosphere is not only far-ranging but also dynamic. It is dynamic because it is continually informed by the consequences of our and others' actions in the world. In our various regions of the world we will not always be doing the same kinds of stewardly activities, but in our responses to what we learn from creation we will often change what we do—all in the direction of sustaining the integrity of creation.

What does stewardship of creation accomplish in our world today? Here's a definition that helps answer this question: *Stewardship of the creation dynamically shapes and reshapes human behavior in the direction of maintaining sustainability for ecosystems and the biosphere over the generations in the biophysical and covenantal context.*

GOD IN RELATIONSHIP WITH US AND CREATION

Stewardship of all these gifts and blessings has been God's expectation of people throughout history. And this expectation comes not as a dictate from a distant deity, but from God *in relationship* with us. We are people created in God's image to relate in communion with our Maker and Provider. Beginning with God's communion with Adam and Eve in the garden and on through the great dramatic history of redemption, God remains in *relationship*—both with us and with creation. This relationship continues also into the future. God's immanence—"God with us" (Matt. 1:23)—sustains this relationship. God's transcendence—God as sovereign and eternal—assures us that the whole universe is in God's hands. This is true from before the beginning of time, and it is true forever into the future. God's immanence and transcendence provide the awesome context of the three-way relationship among God, creation, and human beings.

All of this assures us that we are not mere afterthoughts of God in creation. As imagers of God's love, we are created to care for and serve creation, including other human creatures, on behalf of God. Creation stewardship calls for imaging God's care and keeping for all that the Lord has made. As images, we do God's will; as imagers, we reflect God's glory.

Our *relationship* began when God breathed into us the breath of life and we became living beings (Gen. 2:7). And when God gave us the vocation of serving and safeguarding the garden (2:15), we entered a three-way relationship that provides a framework for our life and living on earth, the framework for stewardship.

IS CREATION A LOST CAUSE?

Many people today—both "people of faith" and others—are wondering if creation, with all its degradations and lost treasures, has become a lost cause. So many things are damaged or broken in the biosphere that we might wonder, "How can any of this possibly be repaired?" Having learned about the degradations human beings have brought about in creation, some might advocate that we "just give up!"

Lest we lean toward that kind of thinking or develop some perverse extension of it, like "Eat, drink, and be merry, for tomorrow we die!"—or perhaps something even worse—we may need to come to grips with our responsibility to serve God and his creation. For most of us in North America, this may mean we need to serve more responsibly than we or our ancestors have done. It is important to hear what Scripture says about our responsibility. And while statements like the following can be quite sobering, especially in view of God's final judgment, they can help us get back on track if we have strayed. Revelation 11:18, for example, states that "the time [will] come for [God's] judging the dead, and for rewarding . . . people who revere [God's] name, both great and small—and for destroying those who destroy the earth."

Of course, it is not only this declaration that affirms God's continuing *relationship* with us and with creation. This statement is backed up and preceded by many assurances of promise and blessing, including what we call "signs and seals." All of this assures us that God does not abandon the creation. Neither does God abandon us!

SIGNS AND SEALS

In the divine order of things, our *relationship* with God, including the promises God has made to us, is confirmed with signs and seals—and these have a lot to do with creation stewardship. One of the oldest signs in creation that reminds us of God's care, for example, is the rainbow. After God sent a great flood to destroy most of humanity for its wickedness, the Lord made promises to Noah and his family, who with all kinds of animals were saved from the flood—declaring that the rainbow would be a sign that God would never again send such a flood "to destroy all life" (Gen. 9:15).

Baptism is another example. Baptism is a sign and seal of being bonded to Christ. It testifies that as surely as we can use water to wash our bodies clean, we can trust through faith in Christ that the Spirit of Christ washes away our sins (Heidelberg Catechism, Q&A 73).

Still another example is the bread and wine (or grape juice) in the sacrament of the Lord's Supper (Holy Communion, Holy Eucharist).

THE WORD MADE FLESH

We stand at a place in history that begins with Adam, moves on to Jesus crucified and risen, and is commemorated in our day in Holy Communion (Holy Eucharist). We have come to know Adam of Eden as "the first Adam." Prefiguring "the final Adam," Adam was envisioned, in *Paradise Lost* by John Milton (1674), singing at sunrise with Eve in Eden,

> Ye Mists and Exhalations, that now rise
> From hill or steaming lake, dusky or gray,
> Till the sun paint your fleecy skirts with gold,
> In honour to the world's great Author rise;
> Whether to deck with clouds the uncoloured sky,
> Or wet the thirsty earth with falling showers,
> Rising or falling still advance his praise.

Despite the immense beauty, fruitfulness, and pleasant atmosphere of Eden, humanity was dissatisfied with the garden's economy and its limits (Gen. 3). Yielding to the tempter—aiming to gain freedom from earth's constraints—became the pattern they set. So their descendants in another day proclaimed, "Come, let us build ourselves a city, with a tower that reaches to the heavens, so that we may make a name for ourselves" (Gen. 11:3). Thinking they could do as they wished with the elements of creation, that all its properties were subservient to them, they believed they could make things "bigger than life."

Humans have been pursuing this "freedom" ever since, "freedom" from God's economy with its life-giving principles and wholesome constraints—and with that came degradations and losses of creation's life-giving services. Gaining the "freedom" to take charge, people became creation's consumers.

The final Adam, Jesus Christ, however, overcame temptation and conquered death, vindicating creation in his incarnation and resurrection. He thus opened the door to a new Eden—the new and renewed creation—meeting creation's eager expectation for the coming of the children of God (Rom. 8:19). As we eat the bread and drink the wine in Holy Communion, we participate in Christ's crucified body and shed blood, thereby vindicating creation and God's kingdom, for which we pray.

Creation is not a lost cause. God's Son has himself entered God's own creation to redeem it and us.

By undoing the degrading works of Adam and his followers, and by leading us in doing what Adam was supposed to do, Jesus reconciles all things to God (see Rom. 5:8-11; 2 Cor. 5:17-20; Col. 1:20), renewing the life of the earth. Jesus is the hope of the world, and we follow him. All the principles on creation care that we have gleaned from Scripture originate, reverberate, and find their fulfillment in Jesus Christ. And so we pray his prayer to the Father: "Your kingdom come, your will be done, on earth . . ." (Matt. 6:10).

A pastor friend of mine summed up about an hour's discussion on creation care by saying, "We should so behave on earth that heaven is not a shock to us!" He is right, of course. But we can take this further to anticipate the renewed earth, for this too is promised (see Isa. 65:17; Rom. 8:19-21; Rev. 21-22). Perhaps we also can sum up the importance of caring for creation by saying, "We should so behave on earth that the renewed earth will not be a shock to us!"

Suggestions for Study

GETTING STARTED

We got under way in chapter 3 by exploring biblical teachings about creation care, and we found numerous Scripture texts that are very useful for learning God's will for us in creation. In this chapter we have built on that work to explore things more deeply and theologically, relating Scripture to Scripture and reflecting on the meaning of the Bible's identification of Christ as the final Adam who vindicates and restores creation.

Scripture Readings

Genesis 2:7, 15; 9:12-17; 11:3-4; 17:7

Psalm 19:1

John 1:1-4, 14; 3:16-17

Romans 1:20-23; 8:19-22

1 Corinthians 15:22

2 Corinthians 3:18; 5:17-20

Colossians 1:15-20

Revelation 11:18

Opening Prayer

We can thank God for the great depth of the Scriptures and for the richness that Scripture study brings to our understanding of God's will for our lives and for creation. In our prayer we can also give thanks for God's gift of the final Adam, Jesus Christ, and ask that we may increasingly discover what it means to follow the one who upholds and reconciles all things.

FOR THOUGHT AND DISCUSSION

What do Christian people confess, and why?

1. A theological statement of faith on the topic of our study is provided in *Our World Belongs to God: A Contemporary Testimony.* Excerpts from this testimony follow (para. 10,

15, 17-18, 23-24, 26-27). Reflect and share your thoughts on how these statements based on Scripture can help us share with others our role as stewards of the creation ruled and held together by Christ as King today.

10. Made in God's image
   to live in loving communion with our Maker,
   we are appointed earthkeepers and caretakers
   to tend the earth, enjoy it,
   and love our neighbors.
   God uses our skills
   for the unfolding and well-being of his world
   so that creation and all who live in it may flourish.

15. When humans deface God's image,
   the whole world suffers:
   we abuse the creation or idolize it;
   we are estranged from our Creator,
   from our neighbor,
   from our true selves,
   and from all that God has made.

17. In all our striving
   to excuse or save ourselves,
   we stand condemned
   before the God of truth.
   But our world,
   broken and scarred,
   still belongs to God,
   who holds it together
   and gives us hope.

18. While justly angry,
   God did not turn away
   from a world bent on destruction
   but turned to face it in love.
   With patience and tender care
   the Lord set out
   on the long road of redemption
   to reclaim the lost as his people
   and the world as his kingdom.

23. Remembering the promise
to reconcile the world to himself,
God joined our humanity in Jesus Christ—
the eternal Word made flesh.
He is the long-awaited Messiah,
one with us
and one with God,
fully human and fully divine,
conceived by the Holy Spirit
and born of the virgin Mary.

24. As the second Adam,
Jesus chose the path we had rejected.
In his baptism and temptations,
teaching and miracles,
battles with demons
and friendships with sinners,
Jesus lived a full and righteous human life before us.
As God's true Son,
he lovingly obeyed the Father
and made present in deed and word
the coming rule of God.

26. Being both divine and human,
Jesus is the only mediator.
He alone paid the debt of our sin;
there is no other Savior. . . .

27. Jesus ascended in triumph,
raising our humanity to the heavenly throne.
All authority, glory, and sovereign power
are given to him.
There he hears our prayers
and pleads our cause before the Father.
Blessed are all
who take refuge in him.

Of whom are we disciples today?
2. Make a list of actions you might take regarding creation if
you were a follower of Adam. Then make a contrasting list
of actions you can take as a disciple of the final Adam, Jesus

Christ. Which of the actions in the second list are things you already do? Which ones could you easily begin doing, if you put your mind to it? Which ones will take a lot of effort, perhaps together with lots of other people? What might it mean to do these things "in Christ"?

What is our motive for creation care?

3. Discuss the difference between the following motivations for creation care and keeping: gratitude, obedience, love, guilt. What difference does our motivation for creation care make?

Are endangered species worth our time and money?

4. A student I knew, after coming back from observing the Kirtland's warbler—an endangered species of bird that nests only in a small area of jack pines near Mio, Michigan—was asked what she thought about the efforts of conservation workers to protect and keep this species. She replied, "That's an awful lot of money to spend on a silly little bird." In response, her questioner replied, "Yes, the price of gopher wood is very high these days!" (gopher wood being the material from which Noah built the ark). What's the connection? Discuss the issues this comment raises, and substantiate your arguments with biblical principles (see chapter 3).

How important is the concept of sabbath keeping in connection with creation?

5. Leviticus 25 expects the land to be given a sabbath rest once every seven years. A farmer friend of mine in Neerlandia, Alberta, lets the land rest every second year. He maintains that this is what his land needs. What do you think of my friend's application of Scripture here? In what other ways can we apply the concept of sabbaths to caring for creation?

Is creation care really important for Christians?

6. Is a polluted world and the loss of species a concern? Is it a concern for your church's outreach efforts to the world? Should it be? Why or why not? To put the question another way, *If we think it's OK to degrade the world we live in, will people trust our message of good news for the world in Christ? Why or why not?*

Would you apply for the research grant?
7. I was invited to submit a research proposal to determine the effectiveness of using bogs and other natural wetlands as "sewage treatment facilities," but I declined to do so on ethical grounds. However, a year or so later, another scientist who had received a grant for this same research called to ask me to serve as a consultant on his project. My answer to him was "No thanks, I don't believe in using Rembrandts as toilet paper!" Do you understand why I said this? Should I have been more diplomatic? Should I have agreed to help?

PRAYER

You might at this point want to express your gratitude for the richness of God's revelation in creation and in the Bible, as well as for the minds God has given us, in Christ, to assimilate biblical truth and put it into practice. You might also want to pray that God will prepare and inspire you to put your knowledge of his will into practice.

Note: The next chapter introduces a mini-workshop you can use for putting creation care into practice in your daily living in ways that can involve your household, church, and larger community. To get the most out of this workshop, you should have anywhere from five to 50 participants. Group leaders especially will want to plan ahead for conducting this workshop. (See also an optional procedure under "Suggestions for Study" at the end of chapter 5.)

05

Putting Creation Care into Practice
(A Workshop Session)

What can we do in our household, neighborhood, workplace, church, school, and larger community to respond to environmental concerns? Once we have looked at this question in the light of biblical teaching, we should not sit passively and watch as God's creation continues to be degraded. We need to act on our concerns; we need to put valid beliefs into practice. Care for God's creation is not only possible; it is vitally necessary in our time. Honoring God as Creator and imaging God's care for creation, we have an important contribution to make toward living in harmony with our world today.

As we proceed, we need to answer some important questions:

- How do we bring together and present what we have learned so that the people in our lives and around us can catch the vision of caring for creation?
- With the vision in place, how can we put what we know into practice?
- How can we sustain the vision so that we don't lose sight of it when other issues come up in our community or household life?

This chapter helps to address these questions, but not by providing a simple prescription. Rather, this chapter offers a technique for mining ideas from interactive thinking among us—children and adults, male and female, rich and poor, teacher and student, urbanite and farmer, leader and group member, citizen and policy maker—and putting those ideas together so that we and our surrounding communities can increasingly become part of the solution to environmental care in the growing crisis we are facing today.

As we become more aware of God's creation and how it is being degraded, we can identify our homes, schools, churches, and communities as "Creation Care Centers." We can seek to demonstrate our responsibility and privilege in being good stewards of creation, showing our commitment to and sharing the joy of living in harmony with creation. Though we might be guided by the examples of others, we will also want to develop plans to meet the needs of our local situation while also contributing to assessment and action on regional and global needs. To help you get started, this chapter presents a procedure in the form of a mini-workshop that can be used effectively. (See also an optional procedure described in "Suggestions for Study" at the end of this chapter.)

A Mini-Workshop

The procedure described on the following pages will help you generate lots of ideas for making your household or larger community a Creation Care Center. It then guides you to choose the best ideas to put into action.

This procedure enables people to bypass initial roadblocking debates about the validity of ideas or budget and time constraints. It also helps bring specific ideas into an organized, coherent statement to present to leaders who have the authority to move ahead with an action plan. The group or community therefore benefits from the undiluted strengths, talents, and abilities of everyone involved.

The procedure works best with a group of five to fifty people who already share a concern for and an understanding of the various degradations of creation. A one-hour session usually is sufficient to identify and screen ideas. Following the session, results should be summarized and gathered into a document for further development and implementation by your group, church, or community leaders.

Because this process begins with particular local issues and uses available local talent, each resulting Creation Care Center will have its own personality, identity, and character.

PROCEDURE

A. General Setting and Room Arrangement

Set up a meeting room with chairs in a single circle. Once people are seated, remove extra chairs so that no empty ones remain (but keep extra chairs handy for any who might arrive after you've begun). Bring a supply of index cards or similar-sized sheets of recycled paper. You'll need three cards for each person in the group. Have pencils or pens available for everyone.

B. Generating Initial Ideas

When the group is seated, explain that a Creation Care Center is a community, large or small, that intends to honor God as Creator and Sustainer in every way. This mini-workshop aims to help people discover how best to accomplish this goal in the community and region in which they live.

To begin, give two blank cards to each person, noting that people should write on one side only. Then ask, "What specific idea can you think of to make our group (or larger community) a Creation Care Center?"

Have people reflect for a few moments and then write their idea on one of the cards. Help group members to think broadly and deeply by asking some additional questions while they are reflecting:

- What is our situation here?
- What local environmental problems need to be addressed?
- How can we become a kind of "window on creation care"— a model of how to care for God's earth?
- What do we have going for us that other groups (communities) do not?
- What special contributions could we make toward the care and keeping of creation?

The purpose of asking these questions at various points while people are reflecting is to help them think creatively. This process can help to free people from real or imagined constraints of having too little money, already full schedules, or the need to "be practical." It encourages them to come up with their best ideas.

When participants have finished writing (after 3 to 5 minutes), ask them to think of another best idea and to write that on the other card. Again ask questions to help people think creatively. Urge them to move beyond the obvious.

C. "Idea Skimming"

After group members have finished recording their ideas, have them pass both cards to the person on their right. Repeat this step so that the cards have been passed twice. Then have everyone read both cards carefully. Tell the group that when you say "Pass," they should pass the card with the better idea to the person on their right. If both ideas have equal merit, they should select either one to pass.

Again give the signal to pass a card—the better of the two that each person is holding. Repeat this process from three to seven times, but not so often that people might receive a card they had earlier. Explain that this process sifts out best ideas by using a screen of different perspectives. The best ideas will naturally endure the screening of different viewpoints.

When you've decided as a group that you're done passing cards, each person should read aloud the better of the two ideas in his or her hand. Without making comments on the ideas, thank everyone as you collect each card that is read. Stack together the "better idea" cards, and set them aside.

D. More Ideas

Pass out another blank card to each group member. (Each person will now have a blank card and the card from the previous round.) Now ask everyone to take into account all the ideas they read as they passed cards around earlier. They should also reflect for a minute or two on additional ideas they could write down. Here are some additional idea categories you could mention:

- use of liturgy, songs, sermons in worship
- building, grounds, parks, streets

- region, state, nation, world
- animals, plants, woods, fields, wetlands
- earth's energy exchange, soil and land degradation, ecosystem dysfunction, habitat destruction, species extinctions, global toxification, human and cultural abuse

Again ask questions to encourage creative thinking while everyone is reflecting. When everyone has written an idea on a blank card, repeat the passing procedure from three to seven times and conclude with the reading of the better ideas. Again collect each card after it is read, making a second pack to set aside.

E. Filling Remaining Gaps

Ask if any of the remaining cards has a good idea that has not yet been read. If so, group members should read such cards and hand them to you so that you can make a third pack.

At this point you will probably be ready to end this session, having completed the groundwork of your mini-workshop. See suggestions at the end of this chapter for a study activity (if you have time) and for closing today's session.

F. Preparing Results

Together as a group (or having two or three persons assigned to this task), prepare a document based on the contents of the card packs. Identify major topics and sort the cards into those categories. Typical categories that may emerge are Creation Care Committee, other committees, administration, liturgy and worship, building and grounds, community, and so on. Arrange the categories in a logical order, with those that address the administration of your Creation Care Center at the top. Type up the ideas, organized by categories, suggest action plans for implementing the ideas, and add a descriptive title to the document.

G. Distribution of the Results and Follow-Up

After obtaining necessary approvals, distribute the document to all who should receive it. For example, you may consider printing the results in a newsletter, if that applies. Follow this by examining each identified category and bringing the content of each category to the attention of leaders, committees, or task forces who can follow up on your findings with concrete actions. Use the document together as you take steps to become a Creation Care Center.

IDEAS FROM VARIOUS GROUPS

Stop! The following list of ideas should not be consulted until after group members have generated their own ideas. For additional helpful ideas in your ongoing work as a Creation Care Center, you may wish to consult this list, compiled from churches and other groups who implemented the preceding mini-workshop.

A. *Creation Care Committee*

1. Form a committee of interested people to advise the church to raise creation awareness, build an understanding of God as Creator, and assist people to become better stewards of our Lord's creation.
2. Publish information on Christian environmental stewardship in your newsletter.
3. Include a selection of books and materials on Christian environmental stewardship in your library, including those with biblical principles, practical suggestions for action, and local natural history and ecology.
4. Provide creation-focused materials for homebound members and residents of nursing homes, including audiotapes of birds, running waters, and weather; provide bird feeders for people's windows, and set up a schedule for keeping the feeders filled.

B. *Worship and Liturgy*

1. Designate one Sunday each season for recognizing our commitment to God's earth.
2. Request a sermon on creation care and keeping.
3. Devote a portion of each worship service to creation awareness and care. (For example, have at least one family report on something they are doing to help take care of God's creation.)
4. Encourage leaders and members to extend the principle of compassion to all living things (human beings, flora, fauna, and the biosphere).
5. Hold a well-planned outdoor worship service on environmental stewardship in a park or in an awe-inspiring creation setting, followed by a picnic.

6. Plan a multigenerational half-day or even two-hour field trip to regain appreciation and concern for God's creation. Include such things as star viewing and delighting in the life of a river.
7. Plant a new church that emphasizes general (natural) revelation—that is, learning from the "beautiful book" of God's creation as well as from the Bible (special revelation). Its mission statement could direct that all members practice creation stewardship and promote and honor the Lord of creation in all respects.
8. Emphasize how each person can give others an impression of creation awareness and creation care in their everyday work and living.

C. *Building and Grounds*
1. Use a building sign that emphasizes the importance of caring for creation.
2. Have an energy audit to find out ways in which your buildings could use energy more efficiently. Become an "Energy Star Congregation" (Google "energy star" on the Internet).
3. Use energy-efficient lighting and switches that turn off automatically when people are not present and when window light is adequate.
4. Assign someone the responsibility to see that all lights, fans, and air conditioning are turned off when the building is empty.
5. Remodel to save energy, doing such things as insulating, adding solar units, putting in a heat-pump water heater, and installing dropped ceilings where appropriate.
6. Research and develop ways to generate your own electricity (using wind, solar, geothermal, or other energy) and perhaps send surpluses back into the power grid.
7. Set up recycling bins for sorting metal, glass, plastics, paper, and so on. Post signs to remind people of your group's recycling program.
8. Hang appropriate banners and wall-hangings in halls and in your meeting area to help raise people's awareness of creation care.
9. Make provisions that encourage people to appreciate creation: windows that open, clear glass panes in appropriate locations

for viewing creation's beauty, trees and flowers planted at points where they can be seen from inside the building.

10. Develop a naturally self-sustaining park (garden) where people of the community can come to enjoy peace, quiet, plants, trees, animals, and the Lord. Have a sign that states the purpose of the park. Plant berry bushes, trees, and flowers that will attract birds and other animals.

11. Add an open-air covered picnic area to your grounds.

12. Add a rain-filled irrigation tank for watering plantings on the property.

13. Encourage people to use alternate means of travel to gather at your building. Aim for a parking lot that has as many bicycles as cars. (Let it be known that in connection with this idea, casual clothing would be accepted and considered appropriate.)

D. Stewardship Education

1. Make use of books and articles in your library that focus on creation care for different age groups.

2. Identify your group's connection to its environment by answering questions like these: What materials make up the products that we use? Where does our food come from? Where does our waste go?

3. Hold a six- or seven-week mini-series to explain the degradations of creation. Most people are unaware of the *actual* problems. Some sessions could be used to develop ideas for righting the wrongs that have been identified.

4. Provide pastors and teachers an opportunity to complete a special course of study dealing with responsibility to God's creation.

5. Develop service projects that involve families: flower and tree planting, recycling programs, adopting a highway stewardship program, speaking to other area groups about stewardship.

6. Serve as a host for children from an inner-city setting for a week. Focus together on the wonders of God's creation, aiming to learn from each other.

7. Involve members in activities that support local agricultural efforts in soil stewardship, such as contour cropping, intensive rotational grazing, reduced chemical inputs, and improved animal care.

8. Fund and support people to act as environmental stewards to debate and influence public policy in the interest of maintaining and restoring creation's integrity.
9. Invite people in your community to be part of your Creation Care Center.
10. Offer community education classes on the how, what, and where of recycling and energy conservation in your area. Become an information center for source reduction and all kinds of recycling.
11. Provide information on environmentally sound practices, such as the efficient use of home thermostats, air conditioners, and coffee makers; the safe disposal of home cleansers, batteries, plastics, petroleum-based products, organic matter—and so on.
12. Make an inventory of all plant and animal communities within a half-mile radius of your setting. Display this inventory pictorially as an exhibit.
13. Organize annual or semi-annual "Creation Rehabilitation Workdays" for planting trees, cleaning up a stretch of highway, landscaping a vacant lot, or buying some land and protecting it.
14. Reclaim a piece of land—an urban park, a city block, or some other area, and take care of it, modeling stewardship and involving area residents. Or adopt a wetland or woodland, keeping it, caring for it, and using it to educate yourselves and others.
15. Take a field trip to a local landfill to show people the waste we generate in our society.

E. Church-based Study Groups, Education, Congregational Life
1. With others in your church, approach Bible study with an openness to receive the message of the Creator on creation care and keeping.
2. Hold vacation Bible school at a local county park, or hold the final celebration of the Bible school at a park, hosting a potluck dinner afterward. Bring students on walks for the purpose of discovering creation, learning awe and wonder, and developing an understanding of caring for creation.

3. Start an environmental awareness and creation care program with Sunday school students, involving them in an environmental cleanup or appreciation project each month.
4. Make creation awareness part of the church school curriculum. Involve adults of all ages in teaching lessons for the children about the need to preserve our world, and provide practical instruction in how to do this. Help children understand animals through pets under their care.
5. Arrange for informal meetings of church families at a local park on a regular basis. Invite individuals who can give presentations on nature to help people notice and understand their natural surroundings.
6. Gather a forum of interested business and science professionals in your church or wider community to discuss and propose solutions for alternative energy sources, renewable energy concepts, and improved energy use in support of creation care and keeping.
7. Purchase glass or ceramic dinnerware and communion cups instead of throwaway paper and plastic products.
8. As a congregation, commit to living out your faith through caring for the part of God's creation in which you live. For example, commit to caring for a nearby creek or watershed, adopting a highway or endangered species, recycling the garbage you produce, and keeping your cars and homes as environmentally fit as possible.
9. Start a program that involves all family members in conducting whole-family environmental and conservation projects in and around their homes and neighborhoods.
10. Have each individual set a personal goal each month to transform talk into action.
11. Hold a Friday- or Saturday-evening retreat that includes nature study and star-watching.
12. Plan a multigenerational tree-planting event that involves entire families.

F. Resource Use and Conservation
1. Arrange to have various meetings held at the same time to conserve heat and air conditioning.
2. Adopt a "no chemical use" policy for lawn and plant care.

3. Adopt a "no throwaway" policy for functions at which food and drinks are served.
4. Use cloth tablecloths for church functions.
5. Use recycled paper for church bulletins, publications, and correspondence.
6. Put timers on outside lights.
7. Put motion- and light-detecting wall switches in appropriate places so that lights automatically go out when people are not present or when natural lighting is adequate.
8. At your church, school, workplace, or community center, develop a car pool or mass-transit arrangement for bringing members to gatherings. Also include bicycle racks. This will reduce the need for a large parking lot and will allow you to turn part of it into a garden for trees, flowers, and other plants.

G. Personal Lives, Lifestyle, and Home
1. Encourage members to make their homes and workplaces into Creation Care Centers.
2. Provide opportunities for all members to commit themselves to stating what they will do as stewards of creation.
3. Arrange for a "pedal-power activity" and use it as a basis for discussing how you can help others, yourselves, and creation.
4. Adopt energy-efficient practices for the use of heaters, air conditioners, lights, and various appliances at home.
5. Continue to show and explain to others the importance of creation care displayed in our lives.

H. Cooperation with Other Groups
1. Search out other groups (churches, schools, businesses, neighborhood associations, community centers) in your area and invite them to join you in forming a Creation Care Center. Publicize what you are doing to encourage others.
2. Form a team to glean from other groups the best ideas and approaches for developing a Creation Care Center, and share these concepts to stimulate thinking and response.
3. Plan a community-wide workshop on God's creation that involves all the organizations of the community. Follow up

with projects on energy conservation, clean-up, materials use, and more.

4. Conduct a city-wide energy and waste audit of public-use buildings.

I. *Providing Leadership in Society*

1. Be leaders in speaking out against the degradation of creation.

2. Continue efforts with other groups in the community to form a task force to encourage concern about environmental issues, and work on things that the community as a whole can do to improve or properly take care of the environment (such as cleaning up a riverbank, lakeshore, or part of a highway).

3. Conduct a study of various occupations and how they affect creation, and then discuss these issues in a community forum, inviting businesses and workers and others to brainstorm about how to improve on or eliminate negative impacts.

4. Urge your community's or organization's governing bodies to make a statement about creation and the environment that offers practical application for daily living.

5. Use the connections you can make with websites to pull together statements on caring for creation that have been produced by other groups or clusters, and glean ideas for stewardship and action.

J. *Yet More Ideas!*

- Build window boxes, rooftop gardens, ground-level gardens; promote other environmentally conscious architecture.
- Build fish ponds with fluorescent night lights for insect feeding.
- Plant edible flowers (nasturtiums).
- Encourage or practice rotational grazing or regenerative gardening.
- Engage in native plant restoration, indigenous gardening, and forest garden techniques.
- Encourage seed and tree distribution.
- Establish walking trails through woodlands, fields, and gardens; include signs that identify tree and plant varieties.
- Restore habitats around homes to provide for a large diversity of creatures.

- Develop lawns with biodiversity that fix their own atmospheric nitrogen and naturally recycle thatch.
- Assist on a farm; buy the meat you eat "on the hoof" and have it processed.
- Purchase a hundred acres of tropical rainforest for preservation.
- Give environmental stewardship awards to deserving members of the community.
- Develop a paid summer stewardship mission experience for young people at the wages they might earn as a fast-food clerk.
- Make your setting a distribution center for native flowers and trees on Arbor Day.
- Make your setting a distribution center for vegetable seeds and related literature on food and the environment in late spring.
- Talk with a farmer about planting a crop for direct human consumption; help identify a market for it; direct any surplus food to a local food pantry.
- Develop a wheelchair nature loop at a retirement or nursing home.
- Conduct a food-source or hunger awareness dinner at church.
- Encourage a local restaurant to use placemats that show the relationship of menu items to the places where food is grown.
- Encourage a local newspaper to get involved in environmental issues.
- Organize the restoration of native vegetation along a stretch of roadside.
- Discuss the difference between tree planting and forest restoration and follow it with a restoration project.
- Buy a worn-out piece of land and redeem it for productive gardening or reestablishment of native species.
- Arrange for an "astronomy night" to help make Psalm 19 come alive.
- Spend a half-hour or more in autumn lying on a forest floor, listening to leaves fall, and observing woodland creatures.

Suggestions for Study

GETTING STARTED

This chapter provides a fresh twist in our study by giving us ideas on doing something practical and important for the good of God's creation. We have come to the point where we can take what we have learned about creation care and develop a practical response. This response will help us specify how we can begin making our church, household, or larger community into a Creation Care Center.

Scripture Reading
Psalm 96

Opening Prayer
As you begin today's workshop you might pray that your group and larger community will become more aware of creation and make practical changes in order to serve God and creation more faithfully in thought, word, and deed. You might also be inspired to pray that we might always conduct our lives in such a way that we image God's love for creation.

DISCUSSION AND ACTIVITY

We suggest that the group follow the mini-workshop procedure outlined near the beginning of this chapter; it will take up most, if not all, of your session time.

After using the notecard procedure, invite everyone to skim the pages of additional ideas presented in this chapter. The group may want to add some of these ideas to the ones they've already included in the stacks of notecards. Please be sure to appoint a subgroup to do the necessary follow-up of cataloging, writing, and report distribution.

Option: In place of using notecards during this session, you could devise another system for generating and recording ideas. For example, you could use a dry-erase marker board. Compile the ideas into a document that can be distributed later.

Optional Procedure
For an option to the mini-workshop procedure outlined earlier, your group may instead wish to do the following:

- Skim the lists of creation care ideas supplied in this chapter, placing a checkmark next to those that could work well for your group and setting.
- Share all checked ideas with the entire group.
- Add other ideas that group members generate.
- Go back through each category and decide which ideas you could actually implement.
- Appoint a subgroup to write up and distribute your findings along with an action plan.

Thank group members for their helpful contributions, noting the depth and breadth of interest represented in the ideas.

Scripture Discussion

Group members may also want to discuss one or more of the following questions:

1. Read Psalm 96. How does the psalmist portray the earth—as a living thing or as an inanimate thing? Explain.

2. Select one or two phrases from Psalm 96 and explain why you enjoy them.

3. What is Psalm 96 really about—creation or God? Can the world in its present condition really praise God? Explain. Share one or two other favorite passages about God's work and power in creation and how creation glorifies God.

PRAYER

You might conclude by giving thanks to God for the testimony of the Scriptures and the testimony of all that God has made. We can give thanks too for our minds as an endowment of our Creator and for the ideas we have generated and chosen using this marvelous gift. Consider also asking God's blessing on those who will compile the results of this session, and pray for the whole body of Christ in its calling to live responsibly in creation.

06

Clearing Away Obstacles to Positive Action

I n chapter 1 of this book we nurtured our awe and wonder of God as our amazing Creator, the Maker of heaven and earth and all provisions of creation. But then, in chapter 2, we were confronted with the ongoing and accelerating degradation of the earth that in many ways results from human abuse of God's provisions. We responded by searching the Scriptures and identifying and reflecting on many marvelous teachings on creation care in chapter 3, and we continued to respond theologically in chapter 4. Next, in chapter 5 we made use of what we have learned about creation and being "earthwise" to generate an organized list of specific ideas for action. Now we are ready to act on what we know and believe! But there may yet be a few obstacles to clear away before we begin.

We know there are lots of things we should do in life, including taking care of the creation God has given us. But often we just don't do many of the things we know we should do. In many cases, there are reasons for this. Some things get in our way and make us stumble—so much so that we might never get past "square one." Also there can be such big holes in the road that they not only give us a jolt but open up to consume us—such that our intended journey stops abruptly before we get to where we were going.

In this chapter, then, let's identify some stumbling blocks that may prevent us from taking action, and then we'll look at a major pitfall we'll want to avoid so that we don't get swallowed up along the path of creation stewardship. Having done this, we will be ready to put our beliefs into practice.

STUMBLING BLOCKS TO CREATION CARE AND KEEPING

There are quite a number of troublesome stumbling blocks in the way of creation-keeping discipleship. Some of these we have invented ourselves; others have been devised by our friends; still others have been devised by adversaries.

What are these stumbling blocks? Here are some common ones, along with comments that may help us in removing or avoiding these obstacles.

This world is not my home; I'm just passing through. (Translation: *Since we are headed for heaven anyway, why take care of creation?*)

It's true that people who believe in Jesus Christ receive the gift of everlasting life. But everlasting life in Christ includes the here-and-now, in which we take care of our teeth, our hair, and all other parts of our body. We also take care of our possessions—clothes, automobiles, homes, and so on. We do all this even though "our days may come to seventy years, or eighty, if our strength endures" (Ps. 90:10). Have you ever wondered if perhaps learning how to take care of things in this part of eternity might be important for the care of things we will be entrusted with later? The world we live in is much more enduring than our selves or our possessions. So shouldn't the care of creation also be a part of our here-and-now concern? (Review the closing paragraphs of chapter 4.)

Caring for creation gets us too close to the New Age movement. (Translation: *I don't want people to think I'm a New Ager. Isn't concern for the environment and working for a better world what New Age is all about?*)

For thousands of years now, believers have looked forward to the coming of the kingdom of God, and that includes the renewal of God's created world (Rom. 8:19-22; Rev. 21-22). As we have noted in earlier chapters, the Bible also makes clear that human beings are earth's caretakers (Gen. 1:27-30; 2:15). As Christians, we confess that our entire earth belongs to God. It is not the private property of any group.

Respecting creation gets us too close to pantheism. (Translation: *If you care for plants and animals, and especially if you value protecting endangered species, you are close to worshiping them as gods.*)

Surprisingly, pantheism (the belief that God is in all things and that all things are in God) is a growing problem even in our scientific age. In our study of creation, we must be careful to worship the Creator, not the creation; we must be clear in conveying the good news that God is the Creator, Sustainer, and Redeemer, and that the awe and wonder we develop from the study of creation is praise for the Maker of all things. But this does not mean we may avoid taking care of creation. The example of Noah is instructive: Noah cared for the creatures on the ark, preserving all the species endangered by the flood—not because they were gods but because God required it (Gen. 7:13-16).

We need to avoid anything that looks like political correctness. (Translation: *Being "politically correct" these days means being pro-abortion and pro-environment, and I'll have nothing to do with that.*)

The Ku Klux Klan, a racist organization in the United States, uses the symbol of the cross in its terrorizing activities. Does this mean that Christians no longer should use the symbol of the cross in their churches? Some alternative religious and lifestyle groups use the symbol of the rainbow in their literature. Does this mean that Christians should stop using this symbol in their educational materials? People who identify themselves as "politically correct" may advocate for saving certain species from extinction. Does this mean that Christians should not act to preserve God's living creatures? We approach the subject of caring for creation as God's stewards, not as members of a politically correct group.

There are too many worldly people out there doing environmental things. (Translation: *If people who don't share my beliefs in God and Jesus Christ are working to save the earth, I know it can't be right for me.*)

117

In Isaiah 45:1-6 we read that unbelieving Cyrus was anointed to do God's work. Often if God's people are unwilling or unable to do God's work, God sees to it that the work gets done anyway. So if some people who do not believe in God are out there clearly doing God's work, those of us who are Christians should be glad for the help and not use this fact to excuse ourselves from our God-given task as stewards of God's creation.

Caring for creation will lead to world government. (Translation: *If we try to tackle global environmental problems, we'll have to cooperate with other nations, and that will help set the stage for world government.*)

There is no doubt that cooperation (with unbelievers and with other nations) will be necessary in order to address many environmental concerns. Migrating birds, for example, do not recognize international boundaries. Their care may involve the cooperation of many nations along their migratory path. Such cooperation does not have to lead to world government. For example, the work of the International Crane Foundation to care for wetland habitats and birds has been accomplished through cooperation between Russia and China and between North Korea and South Korea. The end result has not been a merging of these nation's governments.

Before you know it, we will have to support abortion. (Translation: *Because of the relationship between environmental degradation and growing human population, we will soon find ourselves having to accept abortion as a solution to environmental problems.*)

Our obligation and privilege to care for God's creation does not give us license to use any means at our disposal to address environmental problems. The fact that many people justify abortion as a population-growth control does not mean that people who are convicted of a God-given responsibility of stewardship should not work to care for the earth, including its population problems.

I don't want to be an extremist or alarmist. (Translation: *I want to be considered normal and not some kind of prophet of gloom and doom.*)

Gloom and doom are not necessary components of the message about caring for creation. Frightening ourselves into action is far less preferable than caring for creation out of gratitude and love for God. As for being called an alarmist, is it wrong to sound the fire alarm when a building is burning? In many cases today it may be necessary to sound the alarm.

Dominion over creation means oppressive domination. (Translation: *I think the Bible says we have the right to destroy things that get in our way; that's what dominion is all about.*)

Many critics of the Bible have pointed to Genesis 1:28 (in the King James and Revised Standard versions, among others, which translate *radah* as "have dominion") to show that it is the root cause of environmental problems. But dominion as outright oppression is not advocated or condoned by Scripture. This passage must be understood not in isolation but in the context of the rest of the Bible, which shows that dominion means responsible stewardship. Having dominion over creation is an important aspect of being made in God's image. Part of our human dignity is tied to God's entrusting us with stewardship over creation.

People are more important than the environment. (Translation: *I'm for people, and that means that people are more important than saving species of plants and animals. If anything is endangered, it is people, not Furbish louseworts or snail darters.*)

We often hear this rationalization for not saving living species threatened with extinction. But again we must ask, "What does the Bible teach?" Recall the account of the flood in Genesis 6-9. Who perishes? Who is saved? Are species less important than individual people? At the very least, care for living species cannot be disregarded because of the importance of people. Christ's redemption covers all creation, not just humans.

We must tell "both sides" of environmental issues. (Translation: *There are always two sides to an argument, so if my own views against environmentalism are being attacked, I should be able to find support to protect my interests.*)

There is present among us a concerted effort to promote doubt and uncertainty whenever it helps maintain sinful structures and institutions fueled mainly by greed. The most familiar of such efforts is that of the tobacco industry, which, even after extensive and conclusive evidence showing that smoking produces lung cancer and other disease, has sustained a campaign that intentionally confuses the issues and fosters a distrust of cancer research. As a result, this powerful industry protects its markets for a product that degrades and destroys the human body. The tobacco industry has been used as a very successful model for similar efforts drawing high levels of funding to discredit the science of climatology and its findings on global climate change. A major strategy for promoting the discredit of science is to seek any contrary opinions, dress them up in scientific garb, magnify them, put them on display, and inject them into "debates" to generate distrust, confusion, and dissent.

Science is necessarily suspect. (Translation: *Science teaches atheism, and because I am against atheism I am also against science.*)

Promoters of doubt about the findings of climatology and environmental science have become expert in playing on the fears and apprehensions of the public. In so doing they have discovered that linking science with the question of the origins of life and with evolution will cast a pall on all science, regardless of whether it has to do with origins or evolution. The result is an assault on science as a principal way of learning how the world works. The integrity of science that pursues knowledge about the world is based on careful statements of findings, including uncertainties. This tentativeness of science—which is one of its principal features—is preyed upon by detractors to discredit this highly disciplined and remarkably credible truth-seeking enterprise. In addition, many influential scientists are committed Christians.

A PITFALL TO CREATION CARE AND KEEPING

Beyond the stumbling blocks we have noted, there are also pitfalls that can prevent us from becoming stewards of our Lord's creation. One of these is particularly effective and can seriously mislead and trap us, making us believe we are doing the real thing while eroding and damaging our own life and our ability to be stewards of God's earth.

Across Christendom there is a widely held belief in two major revelations through which we come to know God: special revelation and natural (or general) revelation. Special revelation is the revelation of God in Scripture, the Bible, made up of both the Old and New Testaments. Natural revelation is the revelation of God in the creation—the entire created universe of which we are a part. Through natural revelation we discover that God is the author of creation. We could call the created world and the written Word the "two books" of God's revelation.

Most Christians affirm this "two-book" approach to divine revelation. But there have always been some "one-book" Christians who have seen the Bible, or special revelation, as the only way by which God reveals himself to us. They usually do not remain "one-book" Christians for long because the Bible itself affirms general revelation (Ps. 19:1; Acts 14:17; Rom. 1:20).

Some people, however, who are familiar with parts of the Bible and perhaps have grown up in Jewish or Christian communities, have become so impressed with the natural sciences and how the world works that they have come to believe the natural world is the only revelation that has ultimate meaning. They too have become "one-book" people. Some who believe this way consider themselves "post-Christian." They acknowledge their roots and their "journey" through Christianity, but they see themselves as having passed through such thinking. Some of these "one-book" believers see the Bible as a major stumbling block to living rightly on the earth today, and they insist that the Bible should be dismissed as totally irrelevant.

But there are some remarkably easy ways to avoid this pitfall:

- Continue to pray to God our Father in the name of Jesus Christ.
- Continue to read and believe God's written Word.
- Continue to be willing to be led by the Holy Spirit in our daily walk.

While we must be respectful and compassionate to all who seek to care for God's creation, we must also equip ourselves with the resources we have available, including the power of biblical teaching, to do the work that needs to be done.

NOW WHAT MUST WE DO?

What must we do about creation? The simple yet profound response to this question is this: "Love God as Redeemer *and* Creator, acknowledge God's love for all creation, and act upon this by following Jesus—the one who created, upholds, and reconciles all things."

But a serious problem remains: it is difficult to love, uphold, and care for a world that we really do not know. Thus many will first have to become aware of creation and its God-declared goodness. As believers in Christ, we are called to share this good news and invite others to come to know the one true personal God and Savior, and to have them join us in working to live in harmony with creation and to spread the joy of such fruitful living.

Once we are aware of creation and God's love for the world, we can move on to appreciation and stewardship.

Our ultimate purpose is to honor God as Creator in such a way that Christian environmental stewardship—caring for creation—is part and parcel of everything we do. Our goal is to make "tending the garden"—our striving to safeguard and renew the life of all creation—an unquestioned and all-pervasive part of our service to each other, to our community, to God's world.

We can move in our response from awareness, to appreciation, to stewardship, as follows.

Awareness

In a time when so much calls for our attention—international affairs, local politics, our work or schooling, family needs, church commitments, and other busyness—we might only barely notice the natural and environmental aspects of creation in our surroundings. We might take time to notice and learn things about creation only when we have a day off or when we take a vacation trip—and even then our impressions may be seriously obscured. We must consciously make ourselves aware of what is happening in God's creation.

Awareness involves seeing, naming, identifying, and locating different parts of God's creation. It means taking off blinders that we or society may put on us to keep us focused on our pursuits in life. It means providing ourselves with enough quiet, reflection, and learning time that we can notice and identify a tree or mountain, bird or river. It means entering the natural world intentionally in order to locate and find God's creatures that we sing about in a favorite doxology: "Praise God . . . all creatures here below."

Appreciation

From awareness comes appreciation; we cannot appreciate something we are unaware of. At the very least, appreciation means tolerating what we are aware of. We may tolerate, for example, worms and hyenas. But appreciation can also involve respect. We certainly respect a large bear, but we can also develop respect for a lowly worm as we learn of its critical importance to the rest of creation. We can move, as well, from toleration to respect to valuing. The earth and everything in it has value because God made it so. As we become aware of the order of creation, we will image God's valuing of all his works. And this will build even further until we even esteem and cherish much of what we discover.

Stewardship

Appreciation must lead to stewardship. Stewardship takes us beyond appreciation to restoration. We now work for the restoration of what has been degraded in the past.

Beyond restoration, stewardship means serving. As we understand that God through creation is in so many ways serving us, we grow to willingly return this service with our own. This service includes a loving and caring keeping of what God has given us to hold in trust. And our service in creation will eventually involve entrusting others with what we have served, kept, and restored.

Christian environmental stewardship—our loving care and keeping of creation—is a central, joyful part of the human task. As communities of God's stewards—as the worldwide body of the one who redeems and reconciles all things—our churches and our lives can and must be vibrant testimonies to our Redeemer and Creator.

> "You are worthy, our Lord and God, to receive glory and honor and power, for you created all things, and by your will they were created and have their being."
>
> —Revelation 4:11

Suggestions for Study

GETTING STARTED

Through this book we have discovered what we can do in our household, workplace, school, church, neighborhood, and wider community to care for God's creation, and now we have to face up to a very real problem. We can be easily distracted and sidetracked from putting what we know into practice. This chapter explores some aspects of this problem by discussing stumbling blocks and pitfalls, and this gives us an opportunity to explore our own reasons for not acting. As a result, this chapter aims to help us clear the way to act on our beliefs as stewards of our Lord's creation, to the praise and glory of our Creator.

Scripture Readings

Ezekiel 33:1-20

Romans 7:15-25

Ephesians 4:14-24

James 1:22-25

Revelation 4:11

Opening Prayer

A good way to begin is to pray that all of us may be inspired to be faithful stewards of God's creation without getting sidetracked or tripped up by distractions. You also will want to pray for the ability to discern what is right, and to ask that others might not be misled but rather guided to acknowledge and respect their Creator in thought and word and in concrete, meaningful actions.

FOR THOUGHT AND DISCUSSION

How should we understand ourselves and others?

1. Why don't we always do what we believe we should do? Given what you have read in this chapter, and thinking through what you know from Scripture, ask and discuss this question: "Why is it that so often we don't do what we know we should, and we do what we know we shouldn't?" (See Romans 7:15-25.)

2. How do we relate to people whose beliefs are different from ours? New Age, relativism, pantheism, political correctness, worldly environmentalism—the list goes on. Given the true teachings of the Bible, how are we expected to relate to people who believe differently than we do? Do we have any responsibility toward them? Explain.

3. How can we deal with environmental problems that require cooperation with people from other nations and other faiths? Should we cooperate with others on these matters? Can we preserve our own faith in the process? Should we? What must we do?

How should we regard other obstacles?
4. What about population? Do Christians have to be concerned with the number of people on earth? With the consumption per person? Why or why not?

5. What do we do with alarmists and prophets of gloom and doom? Prophets and prophecy occur throughout the Scriptures. What does the Bible teach us about the importance of prophets? Were any of them alarmists? What does Ezekiel 33:1-20 tell us, and is this at all relevant for us today? Why or why not?

6. What about dominion? Douglas John Hall wrote a book titled *Imaging God: Dominion as Service.* From what we have learned together, explain the meaning of this title. Consider also the title of a book by Matthew Scully: *Dominion: The Power of Man, the Suffering of Animals, and the Call to Mercy.* Perhaps you have read these books. If so, what's your opinion of them? Have they helped you better understand our role in creation? Explain.

7. What is discernment? In view of stumbling blocks and pitfalls along the road to stewardship, discuss the importance of discernment in our daily walk.

How will we now respond?

8. Now what must we do? What is the difference between awareness, appreciation, and stewardship? Can you have stewardship without awareness? Without appreciation? Explain.

9. Do we merely listen to God's Word, or do we also do what it
says? Read James 1:22-25. How can we apply this passage to
environmental issues?

10. What's the next step in our implementation plan? By now, you
probably have the organized results of your mini-workshop
on creation care (chap. 5). Remind each other of the next step
that needs to be taken, and commit together to follow through
on your important work.

PRAYER

You might like to pray for God's continued leading; pray to be
disciples of the one through whom the world was made and in
whom it is held together and reconciled. It is also appropriate to
give thanks to God for creation and to pray that the Holy Spirit
will lead us to action.

07

Inspirations for Sustaining Life on Earth

L iving in harmony with creation as its caretakers and sharing the inspiration that comes from this living—again, this is the theme of this book. For several decades I have dedicated my life and work to this theme, trying to learn and do as much as I can with as much joy and gratitude to God as ever.

Doing volunteer work with me during a week several years ago was an Amish father and his 16-year-old son. They had come to Whidbey Island in Puget Sound in the state of Washington to help restore old farm buildings for what has become the Pacific Rim Institute for Environmental Stewardship. In their work with me, from early morning family worship, through a day of carpentry and roofing, and concluding with praise to God for another fine day, the father asked a curious question: "Cal, don't you ever take a vacation?" My soft answer to him was "I am always on *vocation!*" And so was he!

In this concluding chapter I want to share some inspiring stories of stewardship. In the past twenty years much has been accomplished in caring for creation—from the local level to that of the whole biosphere. One very important thing we have learned during these two decades is that on many issues we must work together. And for people of Christian faith, I often retell the biblical story of Cyrus, ruler of Persia, commissioned by God to do

God's work. The Lord said to Cyrus, "I summon you by name and bestow on you a title of honor, though you do not acknowledge me. . . . It is I who made the earth and created human beings on it. . . . I will raise up Cyrus in my righteousness: I will make all his ways straight. He will rebuild my city . . ." (Isa. 45:4, 12-13). Clearly the work of restoration can be accomplished as God commissions people who do not acknowledge him. I also often recount the story of my being asked to lead a discussion of the first edition of *Earthwise* at a lunchtime discussion group of Christian people whose work of stewardship was in the state department of natural resources. Clearly the work of restoration can be accomplished by bringing into our public agencies the Christian stewardship tradition and the passion for caring for God's creation. In addition I retell a story about a reception held for me by a school of natural resources at a major research university. After an opening prayer by its dean, this school heard me speak on the biblical and theological content of *Earthwise*. Clearly the work of restoration can be accomplished within major secular universities.

Discernment of God's work in the world is an important part of the Christian task. Often God works through Christians and their churches and agencies to apply principles of environmental stewardship in their community planning and programs. Some Christians have even initiated ecological restoration projects by working with their national forest service. But discernment of God's work in the world also includes recognizing the work of people whose living testimonies announce the one they serve, whether or not they acknowledge him. Our Creator can and does engage more than overtly confessing people of the Christian faith in doing his work in the world!

So in this chapter I am including stories that can inspire us to discern how God works in this world not only through overt action by Christians and their churches and agencies but also through people and agencies that do not acknowledge earth's Creator and Lord. Aiming to discern and appreciate God's good work everywhere and through all kinds of people can stretch us, embolden us, and bring us to greater inspirations for sustaining life on earth.

Inspiration One: Powering and Empowering California
A helpful way to gain inspiration to care for creation is to show the results of stewardship. It comes down to something like "By their

fruit you will recognize them," as Jesus teaches in Matthew 7:20. So in presenting this first inspiration, I do not begin by telling how difficult or how seemingly impossible it is to come to a satisfying, fruitful, result. Instead I show the consequences of persistent and concerted efforts made in the state of California to be better stewards of electricity.

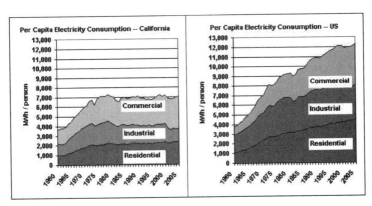

—from *A Comparison of Per Capita Electricity Consumption in the United States and California*, a staff paper by Adrienne Kandel, Margaret Sheridan, and Patrick McAuliffe, California Energy Commission (Aug. 2008; CEC-200-2009-015). Used by permission of the California Energy Commission.

Many people are involved in this story, for which the illustration on this page is a conclusion, but among the most important is a person who became so dedicated that he made a major career shift, bringing many others with him, including the state of California.

If you compare the two graphs on this page, you can see that electricity consumption per capita was similar in California and in the whole United States from 1960 into the early 1970s. Afterward California sharply diverged from the rest of the U.S., keeping its electricity consumption at about 7,000 kilowatt hours per person while the nation as a whole increased consumption steadily to about 12,000 kilowatt hours per person in 2000-2005.

So what happened in the early 1970s? Arthur H. Rosenfeld, "a slight, bespectacled nuclear physicist" at the University of California-Berkeley, became "fueled by a passion to wring the most out of every kilowatt," reported Marc Lifsher of the *Los Angeles Times* (Jan. 11, 2010). Described as "polite and affable, with a knack for making science understandable to people who couldn't screw in a lightbulb," Rosenfeld worked at Berkeley from 1969-1973, tracking subatomic particles by watching the trails they made through a chamber of liquid containing tiny bubbles. But he set that work aside to develop something new in energy efficiency—and the results, which we can see in the energy-use graph for California, are today called "the Rosenfeld Effect."

Steven Chu, U.S. Secretary of Energy, told the *Times*, "Here's a very distinguished physicist who said, 'The energy problem is so huge that I have to change my career.' . . . He set an example for me, as later in life I got concerned about the energy problem."

It was in November 1973 that Rosenfeld made the switch. There was tremendous pressure to build new nuclear plants, and special interests were at odds with threats of efficiency standards. According to the *Times*, Rosenfeld and his colleagues responded with "meticulous research showing that conservation was the bedrock of true energy security," and, said Jerry Brown, who became governor of California in 1975 (and again in 2011), "He gave validation to the very unorthodox notion that economic growth could be decoupled from energy growth."

In the *Annual Review of Energy and the Environment, 1999*, Rosenfeld told his story:

"I was prompted by the 1973 Organization of Petroleum Exporting Countries (OPEC) oil embargo to switch to improving energy end-use efficiency, particularly in buildings. I cofounded and directed the Energy Efficient Buildings program . . . which later became the Center for Building Science. At the Center we developed high-frequency solid-state ballasts for fluorescent lamps, low-emissivity and selective windows, and the DOE-2 computer program for the energy analysis and design of buildings. The ballasts in turn stimulated Philips lighting to produce compact fluorescent lamps. . . .

"When the first gasoline shortage struck, I knew only two facts about energy use: (*a*) the developed countries are expected to burn up half the world's oil in my generation (it seemed rather selfish); and (*b*) European energy "intensities" [per capita, or per dollar of gross domestic product (GDP)] were only about half of ours, yet they had a comparable standard of living. I had learned this from the time I spent at the Centre Européen pour la Recherche

Nucléaire (CERN) in Switzerland and at other European accelerator laboratories, where I observed that my colleagues did not freeze in the dark. They did, however, drive smaller cars and turn off lights in unoccupied rooms and buildings.

"I noted that if we Americans used energy as efficiently as do the Europeans or Japanese, we would have been *exporting* oil in 1973, so OPEC would have posed little threat to the U.S. economy. I quickly discovered that many of my physicist friends had independently concluded that it would be more profitable to attack our own wasteful energy use than to attack OPEC.

"One small incident strengthened my hunch that it would be easy to save energy. At the office, late one Friday night in November 1973, I knew I'd have to wait in a half-hour line on Saturday to buy gasoline. I compared that with the equivalent gallons used by my office over the 60-hour weekend. My too-brightly-lit (1 kw!) office burned the equivalent of 5 gallons/weekend of natural gas back at the power plant. I was one of only a few on my 20-office floor who ever switched off the lights in our offices and perhaps in the hall, but on the way to my car that evening, I decided to switch off the lights in the other 19 offices. The problem was to find the switches. A few were only hidden behind books. The challenge was finding the rest that were hidden by file cabinets, bookcases, and posters. After 20 minutes of uncovering light switches (and saving 100 gallons for the weekend), I decided that UC-Berkeley and its Radiation Laboratory should do something about conservation.

"In December 1973, I had the first of my thousands of contacts with the local utility, Pacific Gas and Electric (PG&E). PG&E had purchased a large ad in the *San Francisco Chronicle* with the following message:

> "'Don't mess with the thermostat. You'll use more gas heating your house in the morning than you'll save overnight.'

"Shocked by this unscientific claim, I called PG&E's research manager Stan Blois, and asked him if he kept his coffee hot on the stove all night, to avoid having to reheat it in the morning. Blois quickly agreed that the ad showed dismal incompetence; and he must have responded quickly, because it never reappeared. But the incident raised some nagging concerns about the motivations and competence of utilities." (From *The Art of Energy Efficiency* by Arthur H. Rosenfeld. © 1999, Annual Reviews. Used by permission of Annual Reviews, a nonprofit scientific publisher.)

Los Angeles Times writer Marc Lifsher quipped in his article of January 11, 2010: "When octogenarian Arthur H. Rosenfeld vacates his utilitarian office at the California Energy Commission this week, one of his final tasks might seem of little consequence: He'll turn off the lights. But that simple act—some would say compulsion—has transformed California into a world leader in energy efficiency."

Inspiration Two: English Farming and Agrarian Culture

We had driven through the Cotswold district of England a few days earlier, and now I was standing before an impressive group of scholars in nearby Oxford, ready to present a lecture on creation stewardship. I had been welcomed to the lectern and was ready to begin with an academic introduction. But I put aside my notes and announced to my audience, "I have just made what for me is an important discovery that I want to share with you! It is a powerful and convicting publication on land stewardship. And yet, while it is very near, it can be found in none of the university libraries in this city!

I related what I had seen in the Cotswolds: a landscape that was publishing and teaching about itself, its heritage, and its history of stewardship. It taught this to everyone who could see: occupants and travelers, residents and sojourners. The road seemed to have been threaded through the landscape by a fine teacher who had important lessons to teach. Beyond the next glade, a small church came into view, fittingly, harmoniously. Settled into its place, it was ancient, rustic, embraced by the graves of erstwhile pastors and stewards of this landscape. We anticipated the next scene because it seemed to naturally follow from having seen this church: an ancient hedgerow bordering rolling pastureland on which sheep and lambs safely grazed.

And next, as the scene seemed to call out for human habitation, a cottage came into view, with rustic people tending the land that cuddled it in contour and vegetation. Harmony led to harmony. Wholeness, fulfillment, was all the scene. It professed to us. It professed what it was and what it had been, the harmony shared between past and present, and something of its fitness within the workings of the greater creation.

Travelers through this landscape have no excuse but to hear its proclamation. Speaking softly with a loud voice, it makes itself clearly heard. Its stewardship message is humbly proclaimed, convincingly expressed, in harmony with the universe. Its context of biosphere, planet, solar system, Milky Way galaxy, and a hundred and more billion galaxies, each with their billions of stars, also proclaimed and published its message. Proclamations by the Cotswolds below and heavens above both convince and convict, though at overwhelmingly different scales.

My comments that day re-grounded my audience in the landscape many of them knew so well. As we also are grounded in the landscape of our own part of the world, I want to introduce another inspiration for sustaining life on earth. Confessing again that "by their fruit you will recognize them" (Matt. 7:20), I present a summary—in the form of a table—of the results of land stewardship in the English countryside. This summary is inspiring not only for what it tells us about farming and agrarian culture, but also for showing us how a dedicated person and his colleagues can develop the motivation and put forth the immense effort to review agricultural practices on nearly two million acres of England's landscape. A keen beholder of farming and agrarian culture in the United Kingdom, Jules Pretty, a professor of environment and society at the University of Essex, gathered data, with his colleagues, on 4,104 UK farms that are designated as "certified organic." While these farms are not as fully "ecological" as they could be, they meet the minimum standards of the United Kingdom as sustainable agroecological systems. Covering about 1.83 million acres (741,000 hectares), they make up "a defined and certified system of agricultural production that seeks to promote and understand ecosystem health" while at the same time "minimizing adverse effects on natural resources." For many if not most of these farms, this performance has come about from "a restructuring of whole farm systems."

The following table summarizes the results of this extensive study. As you pore over the various categories and data in this table, you should know that pesticides now used are "broad-spectrum pesticides" meaning that they kill and degrade a wide range of living things and vital processes and might better be called "biocides." The word *Cryptosporidium* refers to the genus of a protozoan intestinal microorganism found in untreated domestic water supplies; this parasite causes diarrhea that in immunocompromised people can be severe and even fatal. You should also know that eutrophication is overfertilization of water caused by runoff of nutrients from surrounding land and derived largely from fertilizers, manure, and soil erosion; eutrophication fosters the growth of aquatic plants and may lead to the poisoning of fish populations. In addition, BSE is bovine spongioform encephalitis, also called "mad cow disease." Note also that one British pound (£) is equivalent to about $1.60 (US).

The Negative Externalities of UK Agriculture (year 2000)

Source of adverse effects	Actual costs from current agriculture	Scenario: costs as if all UK was organic
	(all figures in millions of £/year)	
Pesticides in water	143.2	0
Nitrate, phosphate, soil and *Cryptosporidium* in water	112.1	53.7
Eutrophication of surface water	79.1	19.8
Methane, nitrous oxide ammonia emissions to atmosphere	421.1	172.7
Direct and indirect carbon dioxide emissions to atmosphere	102.7	32.0
Off-site soils erosion and organic matter losses from soils	59.0	24.0
Losses of biodiversity and landscape values	150.3	19.3
Adverse effects to human health from pesticides	1.2	0
Adverse effects to human health from micro-organisms and BSE	432.6	50.4
Totals	1501.3	371.8

—Adapted from J. N. Pretty, A. S. Ball, T. Lang, and J. I. L. Morison, "Farm Costs and Food Miles: An Assessment of the Full Cost of the UK Weekly Food Basket," *Food Policy* (2005) 30:1–20. Used by permission of J. N. Pretty.

You should at this point do as I do as a scientist, and that is to examine every category and every number carefully, thoughtfully, and comparatively. (No speed reading here!) You will be able to derive much from this table, including determination of whether ecological and health costs of current agriculture are greater than they would be if organic agriculture were adopted in its place, and by how much. You will also find from your inspection that pesticides and their adverse health effects would be reduced to zero, loss of biodiversity would be dramatically reduced, and releases of greenhouse gases (methane and carbon dioxide) to the atmosphere would be diminished greatly—together with water pollution, soil erosion, and human disease.

Perhaps most important, the data here show how the economy of food production can affect the wider economy of human and ecosystem health. Clearly, agricultural practices can take into account ecosystem services beyond mere food production in a program of responsible stewardship. And this kind of assessment can be accomplished anywhere. Does this take work, dedication, and vision to put into practice? Of course. Perhaps you or someone you know has ideas on how this might be accomplished in your area.

Inspiration Three: My Community and Life in the Town of Dunn

Never before had I gone door to door, asking people to vote for me. And there I was, ringing only the third doorbell in my very first run for town office, when a resident said to me, "You politicians are all alike!"

Earlier that evening my family nearly had to push me out the door of our own house with a stack of brochures asking people to vote for me. But there I was, learning to tailor the message of responsible environmental stewardship to each of my fellow citizens.

It was at that third house that I realized that many folks viewed anyone who ran for office with suspicion. It was clear that in meeting with each of my fellow citizens on their doorsteps I had to translate my stewardship ethic into language that was meaningful to each person in their particular situation, and to do so caringly and even lovingly. Among these people, for example, was a mother with three clinging children; to her I translated stewardship by noting that it included the need for lowered speed limits on her street for the safety of her children and the peace of her neighborhood. Another resident was a pike fisherman whose main interest in life appeared to be fishing; to him I translated stewardship to include care and restoration of the town's marshes and wetlands that provided the "nurseries" where pike spawned and their young grew to a size that allowed them safely to return to Lake Waubesa.

Here, then, I present the inspiring story of my own community, because it continues to inspire me and many other citizens of this town of five thousand people, spread across 34.5 square miles south of Madison, Wisconsin.

It all began several months earlier, when I had spoken up at a town board meeting in response to a board member who arrogantly told his audience that they should not interfere with board decisions on land use. He had said, "If you don't like what we're doing, elect someone else next time, but for now you might as well go home." My reason for being at this meeting was to present research I was doing to discover how land use decisions were made in Dane County, Wisconsin. But during the tirade by this supervisor to the dozen or so rather meek people assembled there, I was converted from an objective observer into an emotional participant—leading me to give what later was called "a speech on democracy." Someone took down my name and number, and three weeks later I was invited to a meeting at her farmhouse—a gathering of more than fifty people from all over town. I soon discovered that these citizens had assembled to find a way to come to grips with an unresponsive board and rampant urbanization of the countryside. As housing developments were emerging here and there, our agriculture was threatened, and so were our wetlands, lakes, and streams.

The farmhouse assembly decided that the only solution was to "throw out the town board" by running new candidates for the town offices. That decision resulted in my being elected as one of the two supervisors on the three-person town board in April 1973. Two years later they elected me Town Chair ("mayor"), and soon thereafter the town put into effect a two-year moratorium on all land division to give us respite from day-to-day decisions that was taking all our time. We were enmeshed in a steady stream of subdivision requests and plat reviews, and, while we knew that we somehow had to put these smaller decisions into a larger context, we simply could not. The moratorium, however, gave us a pause that allowed us to think things through, figure out where we were heading, and plan a course for the future.

Three months into the moratorium, things quieted down, and we set about doing a detailed inventory of everything within our borders—natural and unnatural, wild and domestic. We recorded data and made maps of bedrock geology, glacial geology, lakes, ponds, springs, streams, wetlands, soils, woodlands, prairies, archaeological sites, agriculture, historical sites, land ownership, sewer districts, and fire districts. We made lists of the creatures with which we shared the land: wetland plants, prairie plants, crop plants, birds, reptiles, amphibians, fish, invertebrates. We discovered how the hydrologic cycle worked, with all its seen and unseen components, and how we as citizens interacted with it. We discovered the rich heritage of our natural history and social history.

We came to know our place. We liked what we found. We also decided to care for it and keep it. We built a base for a land ethic by knowing where we were and what we held in trust. In terms of what I wrote in chapter 6, we had taken the step of *awareness*. Though all of us had been living there and regularly drove from point to point on our way to work, shopping, and bringing the kids to school events, we really hadn't known much about our place.

In developing our *awareness*, we produced a scientific and ecological description of our place, and this in turn brought us to develop a real *appreciation* for the place we lived and for the landscape we held in trust. Our *appreciation* brought us to develop what we came to call a "land ethic," and this idea of our ethical responsibility to the land, its people, and its other creatures came to be recorded in the *Town of Dunn Open Space Preservation Handbook*. This development then provided our knowledge base for ethical action—for the praxis of *stewardship*. And this action first took the form, in the late 1970s, of a land *stewardship* plan, which was labeled, in compliance with Wisconsin statutes, the Town of Dunn Land Use Plan. This in turn was translated into law by writing the Town of Dunn Subdivision Ordinance. It was this ordinance that provided the basis for deciding how land would be, or would not be, subdivided. Then we took further action by adopting Agricultural Conservancy Zoning—a legal provision for protecting lands that would be kept for the production of food and other agricultural products.

Despite early discussions and debates with a minority that wanted our land to be treated strictly as a commodity to be bought and sold, the large majority of people, who were committed to land stewardship and to the ecological and social integrity it represents, kept the town on course. The success of the town of Dunn in coming to grips with the need to be good stewards of its land and community brought our town eventually to receive the Renew America Award in January 1995. It was the only award given across the nation for exemplary "growth management."

Though this inspiration story—like the others in this chapter—is not a prescription for how to do things, it is offered here to inspire you to find ways to tell or develop a story of stewardship in your community. With inspiration in mind, here are some of the things I and my neighbors discovered in our pursuit of stewardship of our land and our life.

Publication of the Land Ethic in Life and Landscape

In the town of Dunn, Wisconsin, we decided to know our place very well and to act on this knowledge for the benefit of the land and its life, including our own. We instilled a land ethic within ourselves and our community, and we have dedicated ourselves to live within this ethic. We have published it in written documents, but it is published best in the lives of its citizens and in the landscape of our town. The following description was part of a presentation I delivered at Gordon College in Wenham, Massachusetts:

> The publication of our land ethic takes form in the people who dedicate their time and resources to the life of the land and community by
>> serving its people,
>> serving on town boards and committees,
>> restoring its prairies and wetlands,
>> building parks,
>> celebrating special events,
>> producing bicycle and canoe guides,
>> contour farming their lands,
>> planting trees,
>> cleaning up roadsides and streams,
>> raising funds for achieving greater integrity of land and life.

The publication of our land ethic takes form in the land and in our lives, giving visible testimony to the Dunn land ethic in its preserved, restored, and created
  prairies,
  wetlands,
  savannahs,
  woodlands,
  streams.

We have published our land ethic across the town as
  contoured farmland,
  roadsides replanted to prairie,
  a reestablished connection of a marsh, a new natural heritage park, and an annual Arbor Day celebration,
  non-structural flood controls,
  vital and intact ecosystems.

And we have published it as
  a vibrant human community that is integrated into the fabric that covers its soils and terrain.

In the town of Dunn, we have come to know that the integrity of the landscape and the community are worthy of our living and doing. We have discovered that our environmental and land use problems, like everyone else's, are ethical ones. In developing our ethics, we are drawing upon some deep values of Western culture and the longstanding Christian stewardship tradition for refreshment and nurture. These include our belief that we do not ultimately own the land, that we should live in harmony with the land and its life, that we should respect and even love our neighbor, that we should celebrate and provide for the fruitfulness of creation, and that we should not press ourselves or our environment relentlessly.

Often suppressed by the exigencies of "the treadmill" or "the rat race," which so characterize our hurried society, we have chosen to open these values to examination by creating the opportunity to do so.

We learned that time must be made available. Taking a break from busyness can provide opportunity to develop the good sense of so living on the land that we do not destroy it and its life. If we can reclaim a respite from the frantic pace we set for ourselves and others, we will gain the time for asking the vital questions about who we are, where we have come from, and where we are going. We can jump off the treadmill and get out of the rat race to rediscover the joy and necessity of nurturing our land and its life, taking care of ourselves, and taking care for the sake of our progeny and our neighbors.

We found, in our town, a way to bring necessary peace not only to refresh ourselves but also to refresh our whole town in the tradition of keeping the earth and its life, making sure our world maintains its fruitfulness, and making sure we give ourselves and the rest of creation the time we need for rest and restoration. We took this opportunity and through it opened the window that would show us who we were, where we had been, and where we were heading. We found that what we saw of the impending future did not square with who we were and who we wanted to be. This mismatch gave us the incentive to do what had to be done.

We also found that we had to decide to give such high priority to our place that what we do in and for our place has become our way of life. Nothing short of that level of commitment appears to work. So it is not simply a matter of getting the right people into office, or getting the right data, making the right contacts, or writing the right ethic. It is a matter of being willing to change your life so that it becomes interwoven with the life of the land and the life of the community.

Many years later, just after completing a presentation to a class of college students on the town of Dunn, I was asked, "How did you get your fellow citizens to adopt such a biblical stewardship ethic across an entire town?" Their question caught me off guard, because I had not begun my approach to my townspeople as an explicit biblical response to environmental issues. Yet, upon reflection, I knew this was the root of my passion for the land, its ecosystems, and its people. Their question brought me to understand that a commitment and passion for stewardship of God's creation can be brought to a community as "salt and light"—to refresh the longstanding stewardship tradition of our Western culture, with its deep biblical roots, thereby to bring inspiration for living in harmony with the land and sharing the deep joy of such living.

Suggestions for Study

GETTING STARTED

As we engage our calling to care for God's creation, and being careful to avoid being distracted or sidetracked, we grow to be inspired by good models of stewardship, of caring for God's creation. This chapter presents three inspirational models, aiming to help us build on what we believe and know so that we can put our learning into fruitful and joyful practice.

Scripture Readings
Matthew 7:15-28

Genesis 2:15

Isaiah 5:8

Isaiah 45:1-13

Isaiah 55:6-13

Matthew 6:33

Revelation 11:15-18

Opening Prayer
We might pray gratefully to God for the inspiring stories of faithful stewardship in our church, community, and world today—for people who are doing God's will and work in the world, including those who may not profess faith in God or acknowledge the Creator. From a grounding in praise to God we can give thanks for the goodness of creation and for the vindication of creation through the incarnation and resurrection of Jesus, by whom salvation comes to faithful followers. We can pray for the dedication, resolve, and commitment to image God's love for the world in our own life and work. We can pray for leadership present and future that brings communities to care for creation. We can pray that God's kingdom may come, that God's will may be done, "on earth . . ." (Matt. 6:10).

FOR THOUGHT AND DISCUSSION

What lessons can we glean from the three inspirations in this chapter?

1. How might the first inspiration empower us? How would we proceed to move forward on this topic in ways that would show a significant measurable difference year to year for the next ten years?

2. How might the second inspiration empower us? Do we know for our own landscapes what is known for those in the United Kingdom? How can we find out? And, finding out, what can we do individually and together to make a significant measurable difference year to year for the next ten years?

3. How might the third inspiration empower us? Do we know our own neighborhood, town, or rural community well enough to sketch a map of it? Do we know who is in office and what their responsibilities are? Do we know how to run for office in case our service is needed by the community? How would we proceed to move forward on this topic in ways that would show a significant measurable difference year to year for the next ten years?

4. Take a few moments again to peruse the two Interludes between chapters 2 and 3: The Oxford Declaration on Climate Change and Buying Back Time. What might be a good response to each of these, including taking the two together? What could you do personally and in community to "buy back time"?

What inspirations can you detail from your congregation, community, and region? From other places on earth?

5. Can you find or write a description of one of these inspirations to share with others?

6. Is it possible to have someone involved in one of these inspirations to come in to describe what has been accomplished?

7. Could you be instrumental in inspiring others to care for creation, perhaps using inspirations given in this chapter or inspirations you or your friends have discovered?

What next steps should be taken in your life and community to put caring for creation and environmental stewardship into better practice?

8. Review the results of your workshop session from chapter 5. Or, if you wish, repeat the exercise in chapter 5 to improve and refine the list of actions that could be taken.

9. Select a set of these actions that can be combined as part of an integrated program or organized approach and prepare a sketch or diagram showing how these actions can relate to each other.

10. Develop a procedure or plan to implement this set of actions in a way that inspires as many men, women, and children as possible.

11. Write a psalm or prayer of praise, building on the doxology "Praise God, from whom all blessings flow . . ." (see text in Prayer section below).

PRAYER

You may wish to read the psalm or prayer of praise you have written. Then you might also give thanks for the insights you have gained on caring for creation and creation stewardship in your study and life. And to commence your inspired work, you might wish to sing the doxology itself:

> Praise God, from whom all blessings flow;
> praise him, all creatures here below;
> praise him above, ye heavenly host;
> praise Father, Son, and Holy Ghost.
> Amen.

—Thomas Ken, 1709

postscript

Dear Reader,

I hope that this book has been mostly inspiring and uplifting to you. I hope it has helped to empower you and your friends to address the world and its environmental concerns in a healthy, wholesome way—in your community, household, church, school, or college. I also hope you have renewed with me your awe and wonder for creation. I hope this book has been beneficial to you also in growing to understand Christianity's "stewardship tradition" and how it can serve as a gift to the world.

Earlier in this book you probably experienced the stress and frustration I have felt, in having to face up to human degradation of creation and its roots in human arrogance, ignorance, and greed—in short, human sinfulness. But we have now passed through that valley and have come to the highland of participation in the joy and delight of responding in love and gratitude to the Creator of heaven and earth. We have entered the light of imaging God's care for creation. We are affirmed now in our deep-seated hope that God's creatures of whom we sing will continue their successive generations of praise to God.

Today I am enjoying my writing place, at a window that overlooks the great Waubesa Marsh on which I have the joy of living—the magnificent masterpiece of which I am a steward. And as they have been doing here every year for thousands of years, the sandhill cranes are clangoring in wild song! "Praise God . . . all creatures here below"! "Gloria in excelsis Deo"! May they continue to praise God through the coming generations.

And may the Lord bless and keep you, as together we continue to keep the earth in wisdom and joy! May we all commit ourselves to being "earthwise"!

—Cal DeWitt, 2011

appendix
A Short Course in Environmental Science: Sustaining Vibrant Life within the Biospheric Economy

A s you enjoy *Earthwise*, you might just wish to gain a more comprehensive understanding of environmental science, no matter what you already may know or not know. So here is a short course for you! Its essential content will take up to six hours of study, spread out over as long or short a period as you wish. It is easy to accomplish, comprehensive, and fun! Then you may want to engage in some additional follow-up study and creative reflection.

For this course you will need a journal notebook and a copy of G. Tyler Miller's *Environmental Science: Working with the Earth,* 9th Edition (softcover; Brooks/Cole, 2002). Inexpensive copies are available through used-book sellers (especially on the Internet) and local libraries.

First Hour

1. Spend about 15 minutes examining the text as a whole.
2. Read the "Preface: For Instructors and Students."
3. Read and assimilate the first two pages of chapter 1.
4. Examine the "Brief Contents" (page xiii).
5. Examine the "Detailed Contents" (pages xiv-xxi), bearing in mind the "Brief Contents" and the central, integrative themes. Check all unfamiliar words in the Glossary or Index.
6. Note that each chapter is organized using numbered headings, with the first number referring to the chapter and the second number referring to the topic. In every chapter, before the numbered sections, there are a few introductory paragraphs. Move through the entire text and read carefully all of this introductory material.

Take a break to let things settle.

Second Hour

7. Read and ponder every quote at the beginning and conclusion of each chapter and every quote at the beginning of Parts I-V. What is the meaning of each? Select three of these that are the most meaningful to you and enter them into your journal.
8. Identify each of the Guest Essays in the "Detailed Contents" section.
9. Read each Guest Essay, and read the pieces on Aldo Leopold on page 47 and Rachel Carson on page 420.

Take a break to let things settle.

Third Hour

10. Read each of the "Connections" and "Spotlight" text boxes throughout the text.

Take a break to let things settle.

Fourth Hour

11. Determine the meaning of the following illustrations: 1-1, 1-13, 2-3, 2-9, 3-2, 3-3, 3-14, 3-15, 3-16, 4-7, 4-8, 4-13, 4-19, 4-26, 4-27, 6-4, 6-14, 6-18, 6-33, 6-37, 7-6, 7-7, 8-4, 8-5, 9-13, 9-21, 9-26, 10-4, 10-14, 11-12, 11-20, 11-25, 12-11, 12-16, 12-18, 13-8, 13-16, 14-13, 14-15, 14-19, 14-21, 14-22, 14-30, 15-7, 15-9, 16-29, 17-16, 18-15, 19-7, 19-16, and 20-19.
12. Spend about 30 more minutes with the text as a whole, noting things of interest and those things that help pull together the loose ends.

Sleep on what you have read and thought.

Fifth Hour

13. Read the material on homeostasis, page 60.
14. Read the material on Environmental Leadership, pages 37-38.
15. Read the material on Environmental and Anti-Environmental Groups, pages 41-42.
16. Write a reflective entry in your journal.

Sixth Hour

17. Following your journal entry, make a line-sketch for each of the numbered illustrations that are underlined above (in the Fourth Hour list). Do not embellish these, but use line-sketches only.

Now that you have reached this point, you have completed the course! *Congratulations!*

Follow-up

You have finished the course, but just in case you want to continue to think and learn a little more from Miller, you can follow through by reading and reflecting on the following mini-essays and illustrations.

- *Chapter 1:* the essay by Paul Hawkin (pp. 6-7); PATI diagram of Fig. 1-13 (p. 14); and the essay by Lester Brown (pp. 20-21).
- *Chapter 2:* Aldo Leopold and His Land Ethic (p. 47).
- *Chapter 3:* Chemical compounds and matter (pp. 63-65); Energy (pp. 65-74).
- *Chapter 5:* Ecological Niche (pp. 112-114).
- *Chapter 10:* Toxicology (pp. 224-236).
- *Chapter 15:* Love Canal (p. 368); Lois Gibbs (p. 372); the landfill cross-section of Fig. 15-9 (p. 384); Hazardous Waste Regulation (p. 389-390).
- *Chapter 17:* Wangari Maathai (p. 448); Biosphere Reserves (p. 452).
- *Chapter 18:* Passenger Pigeon (p. 460); Blue Whale (p. 477); Endangered Species Act (p. 477-482).

Further Reflection

After this, you might also like to write a reflective entry into your journal.

Again, congratulations on all you have done!

resources

Bascom, John. *Ethics or Science of Duty.* New York: G. P. Putnam's Sons, 1879.

Belgic Confession. Grand Rapids, Mich.: CRC Publications, 1985.

Berry, R. J., ed. *The Care of Creation: Focusing Concern and Action.* Leicester, Eng.: InterVarsity, 2000.

Berry, R. J., ed. *Environmental Stewardship: Critical Perspectives—Past and Present.* London: T&T Clark, 2006.

Berry, Wendell. *The Unsettling of America: Culture and Agriculture.* New York: Avon, 1977.

Bouma-Prediger, Steven. *For the Beauty of the Earth: A Christian Vision for Creation Care.* Grand Rapids, Mich.: Baker, 2001.

Bratton, Susan P. *Six Billion and More: Human Population Regulation and Christian Ethics.* Louisville, Ky.: John Knox/Westminster Press, 1992.

Brueggemann, Walter. *The Land: Place as Gift, Promise, and Challenge in Biblical Faith.* Second ed. Philadelphia: Fortress, 2002.

Cahill, Thomas. *How the Irish Saved Civilization: The Untold Story of Ireland's Heroic Role from the Fall of Rome to the Rise of Medieval Europe.* New York: Nan A. Talese, Doubleday, 1995, 1996.

Calvin, John. *Commentary on Genesis*, 1554 (from the English translation of 1847, as reprinted by Banner of Truth Publishers, Edinburgh, Scotland, 1965).

Daly, Herman E. and Kenneth N. Townsend, eds. *Valuing the Earth: Economics, Ecology, Ethics.* Cambridge, Mass.: MIT Press, 1993.

DeWitt, Calvin B., ed. *The Environment and the Christian: What Can We Learn from the New Testament?* Grand Rapids, Mich.: Baker, 1991.

DeWitt, Calvin B. and Ghillean T. Prance, eds. *Missionary Earth-keeping.* Macon, Ga.: Mercer University Press, 1992.

DeWitt, Calvin B. *Caring for Creation: Responsible Stewardship of God's Handiwork.* Grand Rapids, Mich.: Baker, 1998.

Farley, Joshua and Herman E. Daly. *Ecological Economics: Principles and Applications.* Washington, D.C.: Island Press, 2001.

Glacken, Clarence J. *Traces on the Rhodian Shore: Nature and Culture in Western Thought from Ancient Times to the End of the Eighteenth Century.* Berkeley and Los Angeles: University of California Press, 1967.

Granberg-Michaelson, Wesley, ed. *Tending the Garden: Essays on the Gospel and the Earth.* Grand Rapids, Mich: Eerdmans, 1987.

Hall, Douglas John. *Imaging God: Dominion as Stewardship.* Grand Rapids, Mich.: Eerdmans, 1986.

Houghton, John T. *Global Warming: The Complete Briefing.* Fourth ed. Cambridge: Cambridge University Press, 2009.

Kandel, Adrienne, et al. *A Comparison of Per Capita Electricity Consumption in the United States and California.* California Energy Commission (staff paper, Aug. 2008).

Lifsher, Marc. "You Can Thank Arthur Rosenfeld for Energy Savings." *Los Angeles Times,* Jan. 11, 2010.

Meyer, Art and Jocele. *Earthkeepers: Environmental Perspectives on Hunger, Poverty, and Injustice.* Scottdale, Pa., and Waterloo, Ont.: Herald Press, 1991.

Miller, G. Tyler, Jr. *Environmental Science: Working with the Earth.* Ninth ed. (softcover). Pacific Grove, Calif.: Brooks/Cole, 2002.

Our World Belongs to God: A Contemporary Testimony. Grand Rapids, Mich.: Christian Reformed Church in North America, 2008.

Oxford Declaration on Global Warming. www.jri.org.uk/news/statement.htm.

Pimentel, D., C. Harvey, et al. "Environmental and economic costs of soil erosion and conservation benefits." *Science* 267: 1117-1123; 1995.

Pretty, J. N., et al. "Farm Costs and Food Miles: An Assessment of the Full Cost of the UK Weekly Food Basket," *Food Policy* (2005) 30:1–20.

Psalter Hymnal. Grand Rapids, Mich.: Board of Publications of the Christian Reformed Church, 1959, 1976.

Psalter Hymnal. Grand Rapids, Mich.: CRC Publications, 1987, 1988.

Rosenfeld, Arthur H. "The Art of Energy Efficiency: Protecting the Environment with Better Technology" in *Annual Review of Energy and the Environment, 1999* (24:33-82).

Vischer, Lukas. *Caring for God's Creation: A Challenge for the Church's Mission.* Geneva: John Knox Series, 2007.

Walls, Andrew and Cathy Ross, eds. *Mission in the 21st Century: Exploring the Five Marks of Global Mission.* London: Dartin, Longman & Todd, 2008.

White, Robert. *Creation in Crisis: Christian Perspectives on Sustainability.* London: SPCK, 2009.

Wilkinson, Loren, ed. *Earthkeeping in the Nineties: Stewardship of Creation.* Grand Rapids, Mich.: Eerdmans, 1991.

Wright, Richard T. and Dorothy F. Boorse. *Environmental Science: Toward a Sustainable Future.* Eleventh ed. Englewood Cliffs, N.J.: Pearson Education, 2010.

Young's Literal Translation of the Bible: A Revised Edition. Grand Rapids, Mich.: Baker, 1953.

NEWSPAPERS AND JOURNALS TO READ

Christian Science Monitor

Nature

Science

Bioscience

credits

The chapters in this book are based upon the following papers and articles by the author.

CHAPTER ONE

"Creation's Environmental Challenge to Evangelical Christianity" in R. J. Berry, ed., *The Care of Creation: Focusing Concern and Action,* Leicester, Eng.: InterVarsity, 2000; pp. 60-73.

"Earth's Biospheric Economy" in Melville Y. Stewart, ed., *Science and Religion in Dialogue,* Oxford: Wiley-Blackwell, 2010; pp. 631-644.

"God's Love for the World and Creation's Environmental Challenge to Evangelical Christianity." *Evangelical Review of Theology* 17(2):134-149; 1993.

"Precision of Thermoregulation and Its Relation to Environmental Factors in the Desert Iguana, *Dipsosaurus dorsalis." Physiological Zoology, 1967;* 40:49-66.

"Unsustainable Agriculture and Land Use: Restoring Stewardship for Biospheric Sustainability" in Robert S. White, ed., *Creation in Crisis: Christian Perspectives on Sustainability,* London: SPCK Publishing, 2009; pp. 919-928.

CHAPTER TWO

"A Conceptual Model of Nutrient Cycling in Wetlands Used in Wastewater Treatment: A Literature Analysis" (with Francis Heliotis). *Wetlands,* 1983; 3:124-152.

"Assaulting the Gallery of God: Humanity's Seven Degradations of the Earth." *Sojourners* 19(2):19-21; 1990.

"Biogeographic and Trophic Restructuring of the Biosphere: The State of the Earth Under Human Domination." *Christian Scholar's Review* 32:347-364; 2003.

"Impact of Domestic Wastewater on *Thuja occidentalis* in a Northern Michigan Swamp" (with Francis Heliotis) in Laderman,

A. D., ed. *Atlantic White Cedar Wetlands*, Boulder, Colo.: (Westview Special Studies in Natural Resources and Energy Management) Westview Press, 1987; pp. 289-292.

"Seven Degradations of Creation." *Perspectives* (Feb.):4-8; 1989.

"Unsustainable Agriculture and Land Use: Restoring Stewardship for Biospheric Sustainability" in Robert S. White, ed., *Creation in Crisis: Christian Perspectives on Sustainability,* London: SPCK Publishing, 2009; pp. 919-928.

CHAPTER THREE

"Biblical Principles and Environmental Ethics." *Environmental Review* 3(10):10-16; 1996.

"Christianity: Biblical Foundations for Christian Stewardship" in Bron Taylor, ed., *The Encyclopedia of Religion and Nature,* 2005.

"Ecology and Ethics: Relation of Religious Belief to Ecological Practice in the Biblical Tradition." *Biodiversity and Conservation* 4:838-848; 1995. Also published in N. S. Cooper and R. C. J. Carling, eds., *Ecologists and Ethical Judgments,* London: Chapman & Hall, 1996.

"Respecting Creation's Integrity: Biblical Principles for Environmental Responsibility." *Firmament* 3(3):10-11, 20-21; 1992.

CHAPTER FOUR

"Behemoth and Batrachians in the Eye of God: Responsibility to Other Kinds in Biblical Perspective" in Dieter T. Hessel and Rosemary Radford Ruether, eds., *Christianity and Ecology: Seeking the Well-Being of Earth and Humans,* Cambridge: Harvard Univ. Press, 2000; pp. 291-316.

"Contemporary Missiology and the Biosphere" in Daniel Jeyaraj, Robert W. Pazmio, and Rodney Petersen, eds., *Antioch Agenda: Essays on the Restorative Church in Honor of Orlando E. Costas,* New Delhi: Indian Society for the Promotion of Christian Knowledge, 2007; pp. 305-328.

"Creation's Care and Keeping: A Reformed Perspective." *Theological Forum* (Reformed Ecumenical Council) 19(4):1-7; 1991.

"Ecology and Ethics: Relation of Religious Belief to Ecological Practice in the Biblical Tradition." *Biodiversity and Conservation* 4:838-848; 1995. Also published in N. S. Cooper and

R. C. J. Carling, eds., *Ecologists and Ethical Judgments,* London: Chapman & Hall, 1996.

"The Place of Creation in Today's Missionary Discourse" in Lukas Vischer, *Caring for God's Creation: A Challenge for the Church's Mission,* Geneva: John Knox Series, 2007.

"To Safeguard and Renew: The Principles of Stewardship of the Creation" in Andrew Walls and Cathy Ross, eds., *Mission in the Twenty-First Century: Exploring the Five Marks of Global Mission,* London: Darton, Longman, and Todd, 2008.

CHAPTER FIVE

"Behold the Birds of the Air! The Educational Importance of Environmental Awareness." *Christian Educators Journal,* 2002.

"Christian Environmental Stewardship: Preparing the Way for Action." *Perspectives on Science and Christian Faith* 46:80-89; 1994.

"Climate Care: Our Profound Moral Imperative." *The Banner* 142(4):18-20; 2007.

"Creation Care and Evangelical Relief and Development." Occasional Paper No. 4; AERDO Occasional Paper Series, 1996; Association of Evangelical Relief and Development Organizations.

"Ideas of University of Wisconsin-Madison Students" in Donna Lehman, *What on Earth Can You Do: Making Your Church a Creation Awareness Center*, Scottdale, Pa., and Waterloo, Ont.: Herald Press, 1993; pp. 192-195 (Appendix B).

"Making Your Church a Creation Awareness Center" in Donna Lehman, *What on Earth Can You Do: Making Your Church a Creation Awareness Center*, Scottdale, Pa., and Waterloo, Ont.: Herald Press, 1993; pp. 169-191 (Appendix A).

"Translating Science and Ethics into Practice; Stewardship Praxis: A Case Study of the Town of Dunn." Gloucester, Mass.: Oct, 1996. On the Internet at http://cesc.montreat.edu/GSI/GSI-Conf/discussion/dewitt.html.

"Unsustainable Agriculture and Land Use: Restoring Stewardship for Biospheric Sustainability" in Robert S. White, ed., *Creation in Crisis: Christian Perspectives on Sustainability,* London: SPCK Publishing, 2009; pp. 919-928.

"You Can Make Your Church a Creation Awareness Center!" *Green Cross* 1(2):12-15; 1995.

CHAPTER SIX

"Creation and God's Judgment." *Perspectives on Science and Christian Faith* 48(Sept.):182-183; 1996.

"Creation's Environmental Challenge to Evangelical Christianity" in R. J. Berry, ed., *The Care of Creation: Focusing Concern and Action,* Leicester, Eng.: InterVarsity, 2000; pp. 60-73.

"God's Love for the World and Creation's Environmental Challenge to Evangelical Christianity." *Evangelical Review of Theology* 17(2):134-149; 1993.

CHAPTER SEVEN

"A Christian in Science" in R. J. Berry, ed., *Real Scientists, Real Faith.* Oxford: Monarch Books, 2009, pp. 229-245.

"Community Mobilization: A Case Study of the Town of Dunn." Dane County, Wisconsin: Town of Dunn, http://town.dunn.wi.us/, 1996.

"Inspirations for Sustaining Life on Earth: Greeting Friends in Their Andean Gardens" in Bill McKibben, *American Earth: Environmental Writing Since Thoreau.* New York: Library of America, 2008, pp. 919-928.

"Publishing in the Landscape." *Benedictine Bridge.* Lent 2000:6-8.

"Sustainable Living in the Biosphere" in Melville Y. Stewart, ed., *Science and Religion in Dialogue,* Oxford: Wiley-Blackwell, 2010, pp. 658-670.

"Unsustainable Agriculture and Land Use: Restoring Stewardship for Biospheric Sustainability" in Robert S. White, ed., *Creation in Crisis: Christian Perspectives on Sustainability,* London: SPCK Publishing, 2009; pp. 919-928.